Fish and Seafood
COOKBOOK

by Patricia Hansen

Ideals Publishing Corp.

Milwaukee, Wisconsin

Contents

ISBN 0-89542-616-1 295

COPYRIGHT © MCMLXXIX BY HOWARD HANSEN
PUBLISHED BY IDEALS PUBLISHING CORPORATION
MILWAUKEE, WISCONSIN 53201
ALL RIGHTS RESERVED. PRINTED AND BOUND IN U.S.A.
PUBLISHED SIMULTANEOUSLY IN CANADA

Cover Recipes:
Broiled Lobster Tails, p. 45
Oysters Casino, p. 57
Sesame-Shrimp and
   Asparagus, p. 52
Stuffed Whitefish, p. 28
Tuna-Tomato Taste Treat, p. 8

Pictured opposite:
Bacon Wrap-Arounds, p. 4
Favorite Crab Meat Cocktail, p. 4

Appetizers

BACON WRAP-AROUNDS

10 strips bacon, cut in half
20 raw scallops

Partially cook bacon. Wrap each bacon slice around a raw scallop and broil until bacon is crisp. Serve with toothpicks. Makes 20 appetizers.

LOBSTER APPETIZER BITS

8 frozen South African lobster tails
  (about 4-oz. each)
1 c. Rhine wine
½ c. salad oil
1 T. minced Bermuda onion
1 t. rosemary
¼ t. salt
2 t. sugar
  Dash of black pepper
½ c. melted butter
2 T. lemon juice

Cook lobster as directed on package; cool. Shell and cut crosswise in 1-inch pieces. Combine wine, salad oil, onion, rosemary, sugar, salt, and pepper. Pour over lobster bits. Chill several hours, turning occasionally; drain, reserving marinade. Place lobster in chafing dish; combine ½ cup marinade, melted butter and lemon juice; pour over lobster. Heat to serving temperature. Serve with cocktail picks. Makes 24 to 30 appetizers.

SHRIMP-STUFFED MUSHROOMS

½ lb. shrimp, shelled, deveined and
  minced
1 egg white
1 t. ginger
1 t. Sake (Japanese wine)
1 t. cornstarch
1 t. salt
12 mushroom caps
  Soy sauce

Mix shrimp, egg white, ginger, Sake, cornstarch, and salt, blending well. Fill each mushroom cap with shrimp mixture. Put mushrooms, stuffing side up, on rack over water in pan; bring water to a boil. Cover pan and steam mushrooms 10 minutes. Serve hot with soy sauce for dipping. Serves 4.

FAVORITE CRAB MEAT COCKTAIL

Lettuce leaves (one per person)
Chilled crab meat
Cocktail sauce
Whole stuffed olives

In small nests of lettuce or cocktail glasses, place mounds of chilled crab meat. Pour cocktail sauce over top, garnish with whole stuffed olives and serve at once. Allow 1 heaping tablespoon per person.

TUNA-STUFFED MUSHROOMS

12 medium mushrooms
3 T. butter
½ c. tuna, drained and minced
1 t. minced onion
¼ t. salt
  Paprika to taste
  Dash of pepper

Remove stems of mushrooms carefully; finely chop stems. Sauté stems in butter; add tuna and cook 3 minutes. Add onion and seasonings; remove from heat. Stuff mushroom caps with mixture. Place in a greased baking pan and bake in a 300° oven for 15 minutes or until brown; drain. Makes 12 appetizers.

SALMON STRIPS

1 t. prepared mustard
1 T. butter, softened
4 toasted bread slices, each cut into
  4 strips
1 7¾-oz. can smoked salmon
  Stuffed green olives, sliced

Blend mustard with softened butter; spread on toast strips. Cover buttered strips with smoked salmon. Garnish with stuffed olive slices. Makes 16 appetizers.

CHOICE SHRIMP MOLD

30 fresh shrimp, shelled, deveined and
  cooked
1 c. water
1 T. unflavored gelatin
  Toast rounds
  Mayonnaise

Place 1 shrimp in the bottom of a paper cup. Dissolve gelatin in water. Pour just enough gelatin in each cup to cover shrimp. Chill until firm; unmold. Spread toast rounds with mayonnaise. Top with shrimp in aspic. Makes 30 appetizers.

CRAB MEAT-CHEESE BUNS

1 c. finely grated Cheddar cheese
¼ c. butter, softened
1 7½-oz. can crab meat, drained and
  flaked
24 cocktail buns

Mix together cheese and butter; add crab meat. Spread mixture between bun halves; wrap in foil. Place sandwiches on grill over slow coals and heat 10 to 15 minutes, turning frequently, until sandwiches are heated through and cheese begins to melt. Sandwiches can also be heated in a 350° oven for 15 minutes. Makes 24 appetizers.

CAVIAR CANAPÉ

1 2-oz. jar caviar
  Sweet pickled onions, minced
20 small bread rounds
  Mayonnaise
  Spanish olives, sliced

Combine caviar and sweet pickled onions. Toast bread on one side. Spread untoasted side with mayonnaise, then with caviar-onion mix. Garnish with slices of Spanish olives. Makes 20 appetizers.

MARINATED ANCHOVIES

1 2-oz. can flat fillets of anchovies
1 small Bermuda onion, minced
½ clove garlic, minced
1 T. parsley, minced
  Pinch of powdered oregano
  Juice of ½ lemon
  Tabasco to taste

Drain the anchovies, saving oil. Place fish side by side on a flat dish. Combine remaining ingredients with the anchovy oil. Pour over fillets; chill. Serve on crackers. For variety, add a little celery seed or dill weed. Makes 12 appetizers.

OYSTER STUFFED TOMATOES

1 pt. cherry tomatoes
1 3¾-oz. can smoked oysters

Wash cherry tomatoes and cut a slit in each one. Fill with oysters. Makes 25 to 30 appetizers.

COLD CRAB CANAPE

1 7½-oz. can crab meat
4 sweet pickles, minced
  Juice of 1 lime
¼ c. mayonnaise

Mix crab, pickles and lime juice. Add mayonnaise to moisten. Serve on crackers. Makes 24 appetizers.

HOT CRAB APPETIZERS

1 6-oz. can crab meat, drained
2 T. sherry
1 t. salt
  Dash of white pepper
1 T. marjoram
2 T. butter
2 T. flour
1 egg yolk
1 c. light cream
6 slices white bread

Combine first 5 ingredients; set aside. In saucepan, melt butter; remove from heat and stir in flour. Beat egg yolk into cream. Stir cream into the butter-flour mixture and heat until thickened, stirring constantly. Mixture will be very thick. Pour sauce on crab mixture and toss. Using a small cookie cutter, cut 4 rounds from each slice of bread. Toast rounds on one side only. Mound crab mixture on untoasted side of each round. Place under broiler until lightly browned. Serve hot. Makes 24 appetizers.

QUICK SHRIMP STICKS

4 slices whole wheat bread
½ lb. shrimp, cooked
½ small onion
1 small piece ginger
1 t. sugar
  Dash of salt and pepper
2 egg whites
  Bread crumbs

Cut each bread slice into 4 strips. Combine shrimp, onion and ginger in blender to chop. In medium-size bowl mix shrimp with seasonings; add egg whites and beat until stiff. Spread on bread strips; sprinkle with bread crumbs. Fry in deep fat until golden brown. Makes 16 appetizers.

TUNA-MUSHROOM CANAPES

1 6½-oz. can tuna, drained and flaked
½ c. mushroom soup
1 T. finely chopped pimiento
1 T. finely chopped green pepper
½ t. salt
  Paprika to taste
½ c. grated Monterey Jack cheese
12 halved pumpernickel bread slices

To tuna add soup, pimiento, green pepper, and seasonings; blend. Spread on bread. Sprinkle with cheese. Place on a baking sheet. Broil 3-inches from heat for 5 minutes until cheese browns. Makes 24 appetizers.

Pictured opposite:
Tuna-Mushroom Canapes

SHRIMP IN A BLANKET

6 Jumbo shrimp, half-cooked, shelled and deveined
2 Bacon slices, cut in thirds
   Chili sauce
1 to 2 drops Tabasco sauce
¼ t. monosodium glutamate

Wrap bacon strips around each shrimp and secure with toothpick; dip in chili sauce seasoned with Tabasco sauce and monosodium glutamate. Broil, turning bacon until crisp and lightly browned. Serve hot. Serves 2.

STUFFED EGGS

6 hard-boiled eggs
2 T. butter
1 2-oz. jar black or red caviar
   Dash of pepper
   Parsley

Cut each egg in half lengthwise. Remove and sieve yolks. Blend in butter; fold in caviar and pepper. Fill egg whites with yolk mixture; refrigerate. Garnish with parsley. Makes 12 appetizers.

TUNA-TOMATO TASTE TREAT

4 small tomatoes
¼ c. flaked tuna
3 T. salad dressing
2 T. chopped cucumber
1 t. sweet pickle relish
   Paprika

Quarter tomatoes, but do not cut through bottom. Combine remaining ingredients except paprika, and place equal amounts in each tomato. Sprinkle with paprika. Serves 4.

ANCHOVY CANAPES

4 large anchovies
1 8-oz. pkg. cream cheese
4 T. pimiento, chopped
16 toast rounds
3 hard-boiled egg yolks, sieved

Mash anchovies; blend with cream cheese and pimiento. Spread on toast. Garnish with egg yolk. Makes 16 appetizers.

ABALONE NIBBLES

1 can abalone
¼ c. water
¾ t. onion juice
½ c. soy sauce
½ t. prepared mustard
   Pepper to taste

Cut abalone in ½-inch squares; combine remaining ingredients. Using toothpicks, dip abalone pieces into sauce. Makes 36 appetizers.

SARDINE SPREAD I

1 3¾-oz. can sardines
1 3-oz. pkg. cream cheese
1½ t. grated onion
¼ t. garlic salt
   Dash of Worcestershire sauce

Drain sardines; mash. Combine sardines and remaining ingredients; chill. Serve on garlic rounds. Makes 20 to 25 appetizers.

SURF CLAM DIP

1 8-oz. pkg. cream cheese
1 pkg. onion soup mix
1 c. sour cream
   Tabasco sauce (optional)
1 10-oz. can clams, drained and chopped

Blend cream cheese and onion soup mix. Add sour cream and Tabasco, if desired. Fold in clams, mixing well. Chill. Serves 6.

HOT CHEESE-SHRIMP DIP

2 10-oz. cans shrimp soup
1½ lbs. Swiss cheese, cubed
1 oz. dry vermouth

Heat undiluted shrimp soup; combine with cheese and vermouth in top of double boiler. Heat slowly and serve hot with corn chips. Makes about 20 appetizers.

SEAFOOD VELVET

½ lb. cooked shrimp or white fish, cooled
½ lb. butter, softened
  Salt and pepper to taste
  Pinch of curry
  Melba rounds or crackers

Mince the shrimp or white fish. Cream butter; season with salt, pepper, and curry. Add shrimp to butter mixture. Spread on melba rounds or crackers. Makes about 20 appetizers.

SMOKED TROUT SPREAD

1½ c. flaked smoked trout
 1 c. sour cream
 1 envelope green onion dip mix
 1 t. Worcestershire sauce

Combine trout with the sour cream, green onion dip mix and Worcestershire sauce. Chill to blend the flavors. Serve with assorted crackers. Makes 1¾ cups.

SARDINE SPREAD II

1 3¾-oz. can sardines
  Juice of 1 lemon
  Mayonnaise
  Crackers or toast triangles *or* celery, cut in 1½-inch pieces

Drain and mash sardines. Mix with lemon juice and mayonnaise to desired consistency. Spread on crackers and toasted triangles or fill celery pieces. Makes 20 servings.

CRAB AND WATER CHESTNUT DIP

1 6½-oz. can crab meat
1 8-oz. can water chestnuts, minced
2 c. sour cream
2 T. soy sauce
2 T. minced green onion

Drain and shred crab; remove tendon. Mince water chestnuts and drain on paper towels. Combine all ingredients and blend; refrigerate. Serve with chips, crackers, celery, green pepper, carrot and cucumber sticks. Makes 3 cups.

AVOCADO-CRAB DIP

1 large avocado, peeled, seeded and cubed
1 T. lemon juice
1 T. grated onion
1 t. Worcestershire sauce
1 8-oz. pkg. cream cheese, softened
¼ c. sour cream
¼ t. salt
1 7½-oz. can crab meat, drained, flaked and coarse parts removed

In small bowl combine avocado, lemon juice, onion and Worcestershire sauce. Beat until smooth. Add cream cheese, sour cream, and salt; blend. Add crab; refrigerate. Serve with crackers. Serves 8.

Salads

CAPTAIN'S SCALLOP SALAD

2 c. cooked scallops, drained
2 T. capers
French dressing
½ c. sandwich spread
Cabbage, shredded
Paprika
Lettuce
Mayonnaise

Cut scallops in half and mix with capers. Marinate in French dressing and chill. Fold in sandwich spread. Arrange in nests of shredded cabbage and sprinkle with paprika. Garnish with cup-shaped leaves of lettuce filled with mayonnaise. Serves 4.

BAKED SEAFOOD SALAD

1 c. crab meat, flaked
1 4½-oz. can shrimp, drained
1 large green pepper, finely chopped
1 medium onion, finely chopped
1 c. finely chopped celery
1 c. mayonnaise
½ t. salt
Dash of pepper
1 t. Worcestershire sauce
Lemon wedges

Combine crab, shrimp and vegetables with mayonnaise. Season with salt, pepper and Worcestershire sauce. Mix well and pour into individual baking dishes, baking shells, or a casserole. Bake in a 350° oven for 30 minutes. Serve with lemon wedges. Serves 6.

CURRY SHRIMP SALAD

1 4½-oz. can shrimp, drained
½ c. chopped celery
½ c. bean sprouts
⅓ c. mayonnaise
1 t. curry
1 T. soy sauce
½ t. lemon juice
Lettuce

Combine the ingredients and serve on lettuce. Good with muffins. Serves 2.

SALMON-FILLED AVOCADOS

½ c. mayonnaise
2 T. lemon juice
2 T. water
1½ c. flaked salmon
1 T. capers
2 hard-boiled eggs, chopped
½ c. shredded mild Cheddar cheese
2 large avocados, halved and seeded
Lemon juice
⅓ c. soft bread crumbs
1 T. melted butter

Mix mayonnaise with water and 2 tablespoons lemon juice; heat. Add salmon, capers, eggs and cheese; heat through. Brush avocados with lemon juice and fill with salmon mixture. Combine bread crumbs and melted butter; sprinkle over filled avocado halves. Place under broiler until crumbs are lightly browned. Serves 4.

Pictured opposite:
Salmon-Filled Avocados

GRANDMA'S BAKED CRAB SALAD

½ c. mayonnaise
Dash of freshly ground pepper
1 t. Worcestershire sauce
2 T. chopped green pepper
¾ c. bread crumbs
1 c. crab meat, flaked
1 c. chopped celery
2 hard-boiled eggs, chopped
1 c. shrimp, chopped
Bread crumbs

Mix mayonnaise with freshly ground pepper and Worcestershire sauce. Combine with remaining ingredients. Place in a greased casserole; sprinkle with additional bread crumbs. Bake in a 325° oven for 30 minutes. This is a very light, crumbly loaf. For a firmer loaf, use 2 beaten eggs instead of the hard-boiled eggs. Serves 4 to 6.

Note: A leftover piece of fish or canned tuna or salmon may be substituted for crab meat or shrimp to make up 2 cups of seafood.

SALMON IN TOMATO ASPIC

1 envelope unflavored gelatin
1 c. water, divided
¾ c. tomato juice
2 T. vinegar
½ t. salt
½ t. whole mixed seafood spices
1½ c. flaked salmon
¼ c. chopped celery
¼ c. chopped green pepper

Sprinkle gelatin in ½ cup water to soften. Put seafood spices in a cheesecloth and tie. Combine remaining water, tomato juice, vinegar, salt, and spice ball; bring to a rolling boil. Remove spice ball; stir in softened gelatin until dissolved. Refrigerate until slightly thickened. Fold in salmon, celery, and green pepper. Turn into a 3-cup mold and chill until firm. Serves 6.

PARADISE SHRIMP SALAD

4 c. cooked shrimp, shelled and deveined
½ t. salt
¼ t. paprika
French dressing
½ c. mayonnaise
Lettuce, shredded
12 sweet pickles
Celery curls

To cooled shrimp, add salt and paprika. Marinate in enough French dressing to cover shrimp; chill. Mix in mayonnaise. Arrange shrimp on shredded lettuce. Garnish with pickles and celery curls. Serves 8.

SPECIAL SALMON SALAD

2½ c. cold, cooked salmon
1½ c. chopped celery
3 T. lemon juice
½ t. salt
½ t. paprika
½ c. mayonnaise
Salad greens
Sweet pickle slices

Flake salmon, discarding skin and bones. Add celery, lemon juice, salt, and paprika. Add mayonnaise, mixing well. Serve on crisp salad greens. Garnish with sweet pickle slices. Serves 6.

HALIBUT SALAD

2½ c. cold halibut
French dressing
1 medium cucumber, cut in cubes
1 t. salt
⅛ t. pepper
1 T. chopped onion
1 c. sour cream
Lettuce
Red and green peppers

Flake halibut in large pieces. Marinate in French dressing and chill. Mix the fish, cucumber, salt, pepper, and onion with sour cream. Serve on crisp lettuce leaves and garnish with red and green peppers, cut in fancy shapes. Serves 4.

TOPNOTCH CRAB MEAT SALAD

4 c. cooked crab meat
½ t. salt
⅛ t. paprika
   French dressing
   Lettuce
   Mayonnaise
   Pimiento
   Capers
1 c. cubed cucumber (optional)

Pick over cooked crab meat carefully to remove particles of shell. Add salt and paprika. Marinate in enough French dressing to cover; chill thoroughly. In a salad bowl arrange crab meat in marinade on a bed of crisp lettuce and spread with mayonnaise. Top with strips of pimiento and capers. May also add cucumber cubes for variety. Serves 8.

CURRIED CRAB AND TUNA SALAD

1 6½-oz. can tuna
1 6½-oz. can crab meat
1 c. diced celery
¼ c. diced green pepper
2½ T. diced Bermuda onion
½ c. mayonnaise
2 T. lemon juice
1 t. curry powder
½ t. pepper
½ t. salt
   Bibb lettuce
2 hard-boiled eggs, sliced
   Parsley

Combine all ingredients except lettuce and eggs. Line a plate with lettuce and arrange the tuna-crab mixture on top. Garnish with parsley and sliced eggs. Serves 4 to 6.

MOLDED SALMON WITH CUCUMBER SAUCE

1 c. canned salmon
½ t. salt
1 T. sugar
1 T. flour
1 t. dry mustard
   Dash of cayenne
¾ c. milk
2 egg yolks, beaten
¼ c. vinegar
¾ T. unflavored gelatin
2 T. cold water
   Cucumber Sauce (page 21)

Rinse salmon with cold water, remove bones and skin and separate into flakes. Set aside. Mix together remaining ingredients except gelatin and 2 tablespoons of cold water; simmer over high heat until slightly thickened. Soften gelatin in cold water; add to milk mixture mixing well. Stir in salmon; chill in individual molds. Serve with Cucumber Sauce. Serves 6.

CRAB-TOMATO ASPIC

2 envelopes unflavored gelatin
1 c. cold beef broth, or condensed
3 c. tomato juice
2 slices onion
2 bay leaves
¼ t. celery salt
2 T. lemon juice
1 c. chopped celery
1 7½-oz. can crab meat, drained, flaked, and cartilage removed
3 hard-boiled eggs

Dissolve gelatin in ½ cup condensed beef broth; set aside. In a saucepan, combine tomato juice, onion, bay leaves and celery salt; bring to a boil. Remove onion and bay leaves. Add softened gelatin and stir until dissolved. Stir in additional ½ cup condensed beef broth and lemon juice. Chill until partially set. Fold in chopped celery and crab meat; turn into a greased 5½-cup mold, chill until firm. Unmold and garnish with eggs, cut in wedges. Serves 6.

Soups

FINE ABALONE SOUP

1 1-lb. can abalone and juice
4 c. water
⅓ t. monosodium glutamate
1 t. soy sauce
4 slices lemon
  Watercress, if desired

Combine abalone juice and water in large pot; bring to a boil. Add monosodium glutamate and soy sauce. Just before serving, slice abalone thin, add to stock and cook over medium heat 2 minutes. Watercress may also be added; slice thin and add to broth 1 minute before done. Pour soup into bowls, and place lemon slice on each. Serves 4.

WHALER'S TUNA CHOWDER

3 T. chopped Bermuda onion
1½ c. cubed raw potatoes
2 t. salt
4 c. boiling water
1 10¾-oz. can cream of mushroom soup
1 17-oz. can whole kernel corn
2 T. bacon drippings
¼ t. pepper
1 7-oz. can tuna, flaked
  Oyster crackers

Boil onion, potatoes, and salt in boiling water until potatoes are tender. Add remaining ingredients, except crackers. Float oyster crackers on top. (For thicker chowder use two cans soup and tuna.) Serves 4.

MOCK BOUILLABAISSE (FISH STEW)

1 lb. bacon, cut into small pieces
1 medium onion, chopped and sautéed
1 4-oz. can sliced mushrooms
1 1-lb. 14-oz. can whole tomatoes
1½ c. chablis
½ lb. fillet of sole
½ lb. bass
2 1-lb. cans stewed tomatoes
½ lb. shrimp
½ lb. crab meat
½ lb. scallops
½ lb. clams
  Salt and pepper to taste
½ t. basil

Fry bacon and drain; place in large pot. Add onions, mushrooms, whole tomatoes (mashed), chablis and fish, which has been cut into bite-size pieces. Simmer 1¼ hours. Thirty minutes before serving, add stewed tomatoes, shellfish, salt, pepper, and basil. Add additional water and wine if needed. Serves 6 to 8.

Pictured opposite:
Mock Bouillabaisse

NEW ENGLAND CLAM CHOWDER

4 T. butter
1 c. finely chopped onion
¼ lb. bacon, cut into small pieces
1 c. milk
3 c. canned clams and juice
2 potatoes, peeled and cut into ¼-inch cubes
½ t. freshly chopped parsley
½ t. freshly chopped dill
½ t. thyme
1 t. salt
   Freshly ground black pepper to taste
1 c. light cream

Melt 1 tablespoon of butter over low heat in skillet; sauté onion until shiny. Remove onion and set aside in large saucepan. Fry bacon in skillet until crisp; add to onion in in saucepan. Over medium heat, simmer onion, bacon, milk, clams and juice, potatoes, parsley, dill, thyme, salt and pepper until potatoes are tender. Add the cream and remaining three tablespoons of butter and let simmer 5 minutes or until soup is hot. Serves 4.

ELAINE'S CRAB SOUP

2 hard-boiled eggs, mashed
1 T. butter
1 T. flour
   Grated lemon peel
   Pepper
1 qt. milk
½ lb. crab meat, tendons removed
½ c. light cream
   Salt
1 t. bitters
1 T. sherry (optional)

Mash eggs to a paste with fork; add butter, flour, lemon peel and dash of pepper. Bring milk to a boil and gradually pour over egg mixture. Add crab meat and simmer for 5 minutes. Add cream and bring to a boil again. Just before serving, add salt, bitters and sherry; heat thoroughly. (Do not boil after you add sherry). Serves 3 to 4.

ELEGANT OYSTER SOUP

2 dozen shelled, fresh oysters and liquor
2 T. butter
2 T. flour
1 t. salt
   Dash of cayenne
4 c. milk
½ c. whipped cream
1 T. finely chopped fresh parsley

Remove all shell pieces from oysters. Chop oysters, reserving liquor. Melt butter in skillet; gradually add flour and seasonings, stirring constantly until smooth. Alternately add milk and oyster liquor stirring constantly until mixture boils. Add oysters and simmer 5 minutes. If soup is too thick, add more milk. Pour into heated tureen. Top each serving with 1 teaspoon whipped cream and sprinkle lightly with parsley. Serves 6.

CHILI OF THE SEA

1 1-lb. 12-oz. can tomatoes
¼ c. catsup
1 medium onion, sliced
1 clove garlic
2 t. sugar
½ t. liquid hot sauce
¼ c. butter
¼ c. flour
1 T. chili powder
½ c. clam juice
½ lb. crab meat
½ lb. shrimp
1 12-oz. jar oysters, drained
   Salt and pepper to taste
   Rice

Simmer tomatoes, catsup, onion, garlic, sugar and hot sauce for 15 minutes; strain. Melt butter and add flour and chili powder to make a paste. Gradually add clam juice, and tomato mixture; boil 5 minutes. Add crab, shrimp and oysters; cook 10 minutes. Season with salt and pepper. Serve with hot rice. Serves 4.

CRAB GUMBO

½ c. chopped onion
2 T. butter
1 16-oz. can tomatoes, chopped
1 8-oz. can tomato sauce
1 13¾-oz. can chicken broth
½ t. sugar
  Pepper to taste
1 bay leaf
1 15½-oz. can okra, drained
1 7½-oz. can crab meat, drained, chopped
  and coarse parts removed
3 c. hot cooked rice

In large saucepan, sauté onion in butter until tender; add tomatoes, tomato sauce, broth, sugar, pepper, and bay leaf. Bring to a boil; reduce heat and simmer uncovered about 30 minutes. Remove bay leaf; add okra and crab; heat through. Serve in soup plates over hot cooked rice. Serves 6.

HADDOCK SOUP

1½ lbs. chopped, boned haddock
1 small onion, finely chopped
2 T. finely chopped parsley
¼ t. thyme
1 bay leaf
  Dash of nutmeg
  Pepper to taste
5 c. boiling water
¼ c. butter
¼ lb. salt pork, cut in 1-inch cubes
2 T. flour
  Croutons

Place fish in large pot with onion, herbs and seasonings. Pour water over, simmer 10 minutes. Melt butter in saucepan; brown pork and add to soup; set aside fat. Cover soup and simmer for 30 minutes. Add flour and a little soup to remaining fat in saucepan; stir until smooth. Add to soup, stirring constantly until slightly thickened. Garnish with croutons. Serves 4 to 6.

CODFISH CHOWDER

½ lb. salt codfish
2 slices salt pork
4 c. boiling water
6 potatoes, cubed
3 onions, chopped
4 c. hot milk
  Salt and pepper
6 broken soda crackers

Soak and shred codfish. Fry pork until brown; cut into small cubes. In boiling water cook the vegetables until tender; add salt pork. Add milk and fish, stirring to blend. Season with salt and pepper; stir. Garnish with broken crackers. Serves 4.

OYSTER SOUP NEW ORLEANS

2 green onions
2 stalks celery
24 oysters and liquor
¼ c. butter
2 t. flour
4 c. hot water
  Pinch of chopped parsley
  Salt and pepper

Mince onion, celery and oysters; melt butter, sauté onion, celery and oysters; add flour, simmer 2 minutes. Add hot water and oyster liquor; simmer 10 minutes. Add chopped parsley; season with salt and pepper to taste. Serves 4.

QUICK CLAM CHOWDER

1 medium onion, minced
½ c. margarine
2 8-oz. cans minced clams, drain and
  save broth
2 10¾-oz. cans clam chowder
  Evaporated milk
  Salt and pepper to taste
  Paprika

Sauté onion in margarine until tender, add clams and chowder. Put clam broth in chowder cans and add enough evaporated milk to fill both cans. Add to onion mixture. Salt and pepper to taste; heat. Garnish with paprika. Serves 4.

Sandwiches

PERCH-PINEAPPLE FINGERS

1 lb. perch fillets, cooked and flaked
1 8¾-oz. can crushed pineapple, drained
½ c. mayonnaise
¼ c. finely chopped walnuts
¼ t. salt
10 slices buttered bread, crusts removed
Parsley

Combine fish, pineapple, mayonnaise, walnuts, and salt; refrigerate. Spread mixture on bread; cut each slice into 3 strips. Garnish with parsley. Makes 30 open-faced tea sandwiches.

FISH BAKED IN ROLLS

1 T. butter
1 T. flour
1 c. milk
1 to 2 slices onion, minced
2 c. shredded cooked fish
6 to 8 oblong rolls
Melted butter

Melt butter; blend in flour. Add milk and simmer, stirring constantly, until thickened. Add onion and fish. Cut tops off rolls; remove inside of roll without breaking crust. Set aside. Brush the inside of each roll with melted butter and fill with fish mixture. Cover open end of each roll with some of the bread removed from inside of roll and dot with butter. Bake in a 375° oven until crumbs are browned. Serves 6 to 8.

PERCH ON CORN BREAD

1½ lbs. cooked perch fillets, flaked
⅔ c. mayonnaise
3 T. chopped pimiento
¼ c. finely chopped green pepper
½ t. salt
4 toaster-style corn muffins
Butter
8 slices American cheese

Combine fish, mayonnaise, pimiento, green pepper, and salt. Split muffins in half and butter. Spread fish mixture over muffins and top each with a slice of American cheese. Bake in a 325° oven for 20 to 25 minutes. Makes 8 open-faced sandwiches.

TUNA "FRANKS"

1 7-oz. can tuna
3 hard-boiled eggs, diced
1 c. diced Cheddar cheese
½ c. mayonnaise
2 t. chopped sweet pickle
2 t. chopped green pepper
1 t. minced onion
2 T. chopped stuffed olives
¾ t. salt
½ t. pepper
10 frankfurter rolls

Combine all ingredients except rolls. Split rolls and fill with tuna mixture; wrap each in foil. Bake in a 375° oven for 20 minutes. Serve in foil. Serves 10.

Pictured opposite:
Tuna "Franks"

NEW ORLEANS TOPPING

2 c. chopped cooked shrimp
1 c. chopped cucumber
2 t. minced onion
1 c. mayonnaise
12 slices whole wheat bread

Combine all ingredients except bread, mixing well. Spread between slices of whole wheat bread or on bread triangles for appetizers. Makes 6 large sandwiches.

BISCUIT DOUGH

1 c. flour
1½ t. baking powder
½ t. salt
2 T. vegetable shortening
6 T. milk

Sift together flour, baking powder and salt. Cut in shortening with a pastry blender or two knives until mixture resembles coarse meal. Add milk and blend until mixture forms a soft ball. Drop by teaspoonfuls over casserole, or place on a lightly floured surface, and roll to about ½-inch thick. Cut with a floured biscuit cutter. Place on an ungreased baking sheet and bake in a 450° oven for 10 to 15 minutes, or until golden brown. Makes 6 biscuits.

FISH-SALAD CLUB SANDWICH

1 lb. flaked, cooked perch fillets
¾ c. chopped celery
½ c. tartar sauce
¼ t. salt
18 slices bread, toasted and buttered
Lettuce
3 tomatoes, thinly sliced

Combine perch, celery, tartar sauce and salt; chill. Divide perch mixture between 6 slices of toast. Top each with a second slice of toast; place lettuce and tomato slices on top. Cover with third slice of toast, and secure with wooden toothpicks. Cut diagonally into quarters. Makes 6 sandwiches.

SOUTH SEAS SHRIMP AND EGG SANDWICH

1 c. cooked shrimp
½ c. chopped walnuts
3 hard-boiled eggs
½ c. mayonnaise
Bread slices

Combine all ingredients, mixing well. Spread on thin slices of bread. Makes 4 servings.

SALMON SANDWICH

1 7¾-oz. can salmon, drained and flaked
2 T. salad dressing or lemon juice
8 slices rye bread

Mix salmon with enough salad dressing to moisten. Spread between thin slices of rye bread. Or, mix salmon with lemon juice to form a paste. Spread between buttered slices of rye bread. Serves 4.

CRAB MEAT SANDWICH SPREAD

2 c. chopped cooked crab meat
1 hard-boiled egg, chopped
½ c. mayonnaise
¼ c. minced sweet pickle
Bread or toast

Combine all ingredients and mix well. Serve on bread or toast slices. Enough for 2 large or 4 small sandwiches.

CRAB IN THE GARDEN SANDWICH

1 6-oz. can crab meat, drained, flaked and coarse parts removed
¼ c. chopped olives
1 c. chopped celery
1 c. chopped cucumber
Mayonnaise
½ t. salt
1 T. lemon juice
Bread slices

Combine crab meat, olives, celery and cucumber. Moisten with mayonnaise, blend in salt and lemon juice. Spread on slices of bread. Serves 2.

Sauces

SEAFOOD COCKTAIL SAUCE

3 T. tarragon vinegar
½ t. paprika
2 t. prepared cream-style horseradish
½ t. Worcestershire sauce
½ c. chili sauce
¼ t. salt
    Bitters (until highly noticeable)

Mix all sauce ingredients together and chill. Makes about ½ cup.

TASTY TARTAR SAUCE

½ c. mayonnaise
1 T. finely chopped dill pickle
1 t. finely chopped onion
1 t. snipped parsley
1 t. finely chopped pimiento

Combine all ingredients, mixing well. Chill thoroughly and serve with fish. Makes approximately ½ cup sauce.

QUICK HOLLANDAISE

¼ c. sour cream
¼ c. mayonnaise
½ t. prepared mustard
1 t. lemon juice
    Paprika
    Lemon twist

Combine all ingredients in a saucepan and heat. Garnish with paprika and twist of lemon. Makes ½ cup.

DILL PICKLE TARTAR SAUCE

2 c. mayonnaise
1 3-oz. jar finely chopped capers
1 t. lemon juice, (or more to taste)
½ onion, finely chopped
¼ c. finely chopped dill pickle

Combine all ingredients and mix in a blender for 30 seconds. Makes 2 cups.

CUCUMBER SAUCE

½ c. heavy cream, whipped
¼ t. salt
    Dash of cayenne
2 T. vinegar
1 large cucumber, pared, finely cut and drained

Combine all ingredients, mixing well.

CHINESE BARBECUE SAUCE FOR FISH

½ c. vegetable oil
⅔ c. honey
⅔ c. soy sauce
⅔ c. dry sherry
1 clove garlic, crushed
1 small onion, finely chopped
¼ t. ground ginger

Combine all ingredients, mixing well. Let fish marinate in sauce 30 minutes to 2 hours, or longer. Broil fish, basting with marinade. Makes 2½ cups sauce.

MARINARA SAUCE FOR FISH

2 T. vegetable oil
1 clove garlic, minced
2 T. chopped parsley
1 16-oz. can tomatoes
1 8-oz. can tomato sauce
1 t. salt
   Dash of pepper
½ t. sugar
¼ t. oregano

Combine all ingredients in a saucepan and simmer 10 minutes. Serve hot over fish. Makes about 1½ pints.

CELERY SAUCE

2 T. butter
2 T. flour
2 c. milk
   Salt
   Pepper
1 c. finely chopped celery

Melt butter; stir in flour, blending well. Slowly add milk, stirring constantly. Simmer until thickened. Season to taste with salt and pepper. Add celery and heat. Serve hot over salmon loaf or fish patties. Makes 2 cups sauce.

YELLOW SAUCE

4 T. flour
8 T. melted butter
1 t. salt
⅛ t. pepper
   Dash of paprika
1½ c. milk
4 egg yolks
2 T. lemon juice

Mix flour and 4 tablespoons melted butter in a double boiler. Add seasonings and stir until smooth. Add milk; bring to a boil, stirring constantly. Stir in egg yolks. Gradually add the rest of the melted butter and the lemon juice. Serve with Salmon Soufflé (page 40).

SOUR CREAM-DILL SAUCE

1 c. sour cream
½ c. freshly chopped dill and stems *or* 1 t. chopped dill weed and ½ c. freshly chopped parsley

In blender, combine sour cream with chopped fresh dill and mix on high speed for 20 seconds. Heat over hot water until lukewarm; do not boil. Chill; sauce will set in a few minutes. Serve cold. Makes 1 cup sauce.

WHITE SAUCE

1 T. butter
1 T. flour
1 c. milk
   Salt and pepper to taste

Melt butter; blend in flour. Add milk and seasonings. Simmer, stirring constantly, until thickened.

BEER SAUCE

1 c. mayonnaise
¼ c. catsup
¼ c. beer
1 T. prepared mustard
1 T. lemon juice
½ t. prepared horseradish

Combine all ingredients mixing well; chill. Makes 1½ cups sauce.

GALA SEAFOOD COCKTAIL SAUCE

¾ c. chili sauce
2 to 4 T. lemon juice
1 T. prepared horseradish
2 t. Worcestershire sauce
½ t. grated onion
   Few drops bottled hot pepper sauce
   Salt to taste

Combine all ingredients, mixing well; chill. Serve as a sauce for clams, shrimp or oysters. Makes 1¼ cups sauce.

Pictured opposite:
White Sauce, Beer Sauce,
Gala Seafood Cocktail Sauce

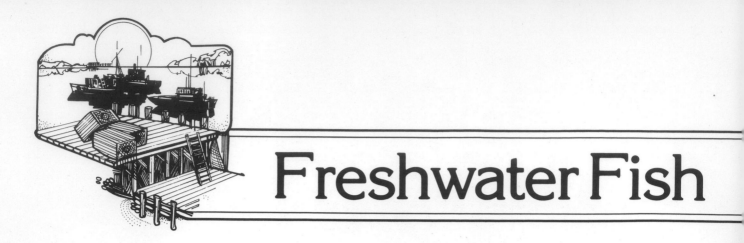

Freshwater Fish

SHORELINE STUFFING FOR FISH

1 4 to 6-lb. whole cleaned fish
1 c. cracker crumbs
1 t. salt
½ t. pepper
1 t. chopped parsley
1 t. diced pickles
1 t. capers
¼ c. melted butter
1 t. chopped Bermuda onion

Combine all ingredients except fish. Stuff fish. This makes a dry crumbly dressing. For a more moist dressing, use stale bread crumbs and 1 beaten egg.

FISH AND CHIPS

1 c. crushed potato chips
¼ c. grated Parmesan cheese
¼ t. thyme
2 lbs. fish fillets, cut in serving pieces
¼ c. milk
¼ c. melted butter

Combine potato chips, Parmesan cheese, and thyme. Dip fish in milk and then in potato-chip mixture. Place fish in greased baking dish; sprinkle with extra crumbs. Drizzle melted butter over the top. Bake in a 500° oven 12 to 15 minutes. Serves 6.

FESTIVAL FISH TOPPING

¼ c. cocktail crackers, crushed
3 T. red wine

Soak crackers in wine. Garnish broiled fish with crackers 1 to 2 minutes before removing from oven. Makes ¼ cup topping.

NORWEGIAN FISH PUDDING

1 lb. raw fish fillet, cut in chunks
1½ c. milk
2 T. potato starch (or cornstarch)
2 eggs
¼ t. nutmeg
Salt and pepper
1 c. heavy cream
Sour Cream-Dill Sauce (page 22)

Put into blender: fish, 1 cup milk, potato starch, eggs, and seasonings. Cover and blend on high speed until thoroughly blended (about 2 minutes). Remove cover and, with motor on, pour in about ½ cup milk, or enough to fill container ¾ full; pour in 1 cup heavy cream. Immediately turn off motor. Pour into buttered quart mold; set in pan containing about 1 inch warm water. Bake in a 325° oven one hour or until set in center. Serve with Sour Cream-Dill Sauce. Serves 2.

FISH PIE

2 T. butter
2 T. flour
¼ t. salt
1 c. milk
2 c. cooked fish, flaked
¾ c. cooked peas
1 T. chopped onion
1 T. chopped green pepper
1 c. mashed potatoes

Melt butter; add flour and salt and brown. With a wire whisk, beat in milk; heat and stir with whisk until creamy. Add fish, peas, onion, and green pepper; heat through and turn into greased baking dish. Top with mashed potatoes. Bake in a 375° oven for 12 minutes. Serves 6.

FISH CURRY

1 c. cooked fish or tuna
1 onion, sliced
2 T. butter
1 T. flour
1 c. beef consommé
1 T. curry powder
1 c. light cream
Salt
Cayenne
Hot cooked rice

Flake fish. Sauté onion in butter; stir in flour. Slowly add consommé and simmer, stirring constantly, until thickened. Add fish. Mix curry with a little cream, stirring to a paste. Add curry to sauce and stir in remaining cream; simmer 10 minutes. Add salt and cayenne to taste and serve over hot rice. Serves 3 to 4.

PIKE ON THE GRILL

2 lbs. fresh pike fillets
½ c. vegetable oil
¼ c. lemon juice
2 T. chopped parsley
1 t. salt
½ t. Worcestershire sauce
Dash of bottled hot sauce
Salt
Paprika

Cut pike into 6 portions. Place in shallow dish. Combine oil, lemon juice, parsley, salt, Worcestershire sauce and hot sauce. Pour over fish. Marinate at room temperature 1 hour, turning once. Drain, reserving marinade. Place fish in well-greased wire broiler basket. Sprinkle with salt. Grill over medium-hot coals for 5 to 8 minutes; baste with marinade. Turn and grill 8 to 10 minutes longer until fish flakes with a fork. Sprinkle with paprika. Serves 6.

GREAT CATCH STEAMED FISH

1 2-lb. dressed fish, (ocean trout or lake fish)
½ t. salt
3 strips bacon, minced
4 dried mushrooms, soaked until soft and then sliced
2 green onions, cut in ¾-inch pieces
3 thin slices of ginger cut in 1-inch lengths
1 T. cooking sherry
1 T. soy sauce

Make three crosswise slashes on each side of fish; rub both sides with salt. Place fish on plate and cover with mushrooms, bacon, onion and ginger. Pour on soy sauce and sherry; steam in steamer for about 20 minutes. Save fish juice and put it in a saucepan; heat and thicken with cornstarch to make a sauce; pour over fish. Decorate with parsley and serve hot. Allow 1 fish per person.

SMELTS IN BARBECUE SAUCE

1 lb. fresh or frozen smelts, thawed
1 6-oz. can tomato sauce
½ c. chopped onion
2 T. brown sugar
2 T. vinegar
1 T. Worcestershire sauce
1 T. water
2 t. prepared mustard
¼ t. salt

Clean, rinse and wipe fish dry. In a large bowl, combine remaining ingredients, mixing well. Marinate fish in tomato mixture, cover and refrigerate for several hours. Pour fish and marinade in a large skillet; bring to a boil. Reduce heat and simmer, uncovered, 8 to 10 minutes. Serves 3 to 4.

FRIED SMELTS

1 lb. fresh or thawed frozen smelts
¼ c. milk
½ c. cornmeal
½ t. salt
¼ c. melted butter
Snipped parsley
Lemon wedges

Rinse fish; wipe dry. Dip in milk and then in a mixture of cornmeal and salt. In a large skillet melt butter; sauté fish in butter until tender, about 5 minutes on each side. Sprinkle with snipped parsley. Serve with lemon wedges. Serves 2.

TROUT AND BLUE CHEESE SAUCE

1½ lbs. trout steaks
1 10-oz. can condensed cream of
   shrimp soup
2 t. lemon juice
½ c. sour cream
⅓ c. crumbled blue cheese

Cut fish into 4 or 5 portions. Place in a greased, shallow baking dish. In a saucepan, combine soup and lemon juice; heat until boiling. Blend in sour cream and blue cheese; simmer over low heat until heated through. Pour over fish. Bake, uncovered in a 375° oven 30 minutes until fish flakes easily with a fork. Serves 4 to 5.

BAKED TROUT

1 large trout, dressed
Salt
Pepper
3 medium onions, sliced
1 clove garlic, minced
3 slices bacon
2 bay leaves
1 1-lb. 14-oz. can tomatoes

Rub salt and pepper over trout. Stuff with 1 sliced onion and garlic. Place trout in a pan; top with remaining onion slices. Place bacon and bay leaves over onions. Pour tomatoes over all. Bake in a 350° oven until trout is tender, about 15 minutes or until fish flakes easily with a fork. One-half pound of fish per serving.

FISH IN SAUCY CHEESE

1 lb. fish steaks or fillets, cut in serving
   pieces (trout, whitefish, bass)
1 T. butter
¼ t. salt
¼ t. pepper
1 10-oz. pkg. frozen cut asparagus
1 10-oz. can Cheddar cheese soup
¼ c. milk
1 c. soft bread crumbs
2 T. melted butter

Place fish in a greased baking dish; dot with butter and sprinkle with salt and pepper. Bake in a 325° oven for 35 minutes. Meanwhile, cook asparagus as directed on package; drain and place asparagus on top of fish. Combine soup and milk and pour over fish. Combine crumbs and melted butter; sprinkle on top of soup. Return to oven until light brown. Serves 4.

HERBED TROUT BAKE

1 lb. fresh or partially thawed frozen
   trout fillets
¼ c. chopped onion
1 small clove garlic, minced
2 T. butter
½ t. tarragon
¼ t. thyme
¼ t. salt
   Dash of pepper
¼ c. cornflake crumbs

Place fillets in greased baking dish. In skillet, sauté onion and garlic in butter until tender; stir in seasonings; simmer 1 minute. Spread onion mixture over fish and top with cornflake crumbs. Bake in a 475° oven 10 to 12 minutes or until fish flakes easily with a fork. Serves 4.

PAPRIKA WHITEFISH

2 large slices of whitefish
¼ t. salt
¼ t. pepper
¼ t. monosodium glutamate
½ c. flour
1 t. paprika
3 T. vegetable oil
1 round Bermuda onion, chopped
2 small tomatoes, chopped
½ c. water
2 T. catsup

Drain fish and dry. Sprinkle salt, pepper and monosodium glutamate on fish slices. Mix flour and paprika. Roll fish in flour mixture and fry in oil until brown. When done, remove and fry onion; add tomato. Add water and catsup to vegetables. Return fish to sauce and simmer 5 to 10 minutes, or until fish flakes easily with a fork. Serves 2.

STUFFED WHITEFISH

1 3-lb. dressed fresh or frozen whitefish
   Salt and pepper
2 c. dry bread cubes
⅓ c. finely chopped onion
⅓ c. sour cream
¼ c. chopped dill pickle
½ t. paprika
½ t. salt
⅛ t. pepper
¼ c. vegetable oil

If using frozen fish, thaw. Sprinkle generously with salt and pepper; place fish in a greased, shallow baking pan. Combine bread cubes, onion, sour cream, pickle, paprika, salt, and pepper. Stuff fish loosely with mixture. Brush fish generously with vegetable oil; cover with foil. Bake in a 375° oven 45 to 50 minutes or until fish flakes easily with a fork. Serves 6.

ORIENTAL STEAMED FISH

4 to 6 lb. (dressed) white fish
   Salt
¼ c. butter
¼ lb. mushrooms, sliced
4 green onions, sliced
3 T. soy sauce
1 t. grated fresh ginger
1 t. salt
2 t. cornstarch
2 t. sherry

Wash fish, cover inside and out with salt; let stand 2 to 3 hours. Wash and pat dry, sprinkle inside lightly with salt. Shape pan of heavy foil closely around the fish; set in larger pan. In a small pan melt butter; sauté mushrooms and onions about 5 minutes. Stir in the soy sauce, ginger and salt; then stir in the cornstarch blended with sherry. Cook until thickened and then pour over fish. Tightly cover the pan and fish with tent of heavy foil. Bake in a 400° oven for 7 to 10 minutes per pound. Serves 12 to 18.

COATED CATFISH

8 fresh or frozen dressed catfish
  (about ½ lb. each)
  Salt and pepper
2 eggs
2 T. water
2 c. instant mashed potatoes
2 envelopes onion salad dressing mix
  Salad oil

Thaw frozen fish. Season with salt and pepper. Combine eggs and water. Mix potato flakes and dressing mix. Dip fish into egg mixture, then roll in potato mixture; repeat. Brown fish in hot oil on one side for 4 to 5 minutes. Turn gently; brown on other side 4 to 5 minutes until fish is golden and flakes easily. Serves 8.

STEAMED CARP

1 3-lb. fresh or thawed, frozen dressed
  carp
1 medium onion, thinly sliced
2 sprigs parsley, chopped in large pieces
1 bay leaf
3 whole peppercorns
½ t. salt per 1 cup water

Pour ½-inch water into a Dutch oven. Add onion, parsley, bay leaf, peppercorns, and salt; bring to a boil. Place carp on greased rack; set into pan. Cover and simmer about 20 to 25 minutes or until done. Drain and serve immediately. Serves 6.

TERIYAKI CATFISH

1 lb. catfish fillets
⅓ c. soy sauce
⅓ c. sugar
1 T. Sake
¼ t. monosodium glutamate
1 to 2-inch gingerroot, crushed
1 clove garlic, crushed

Combine all ingredients except catfish. Marinate fish in sauce for 1 hour. Broil over charcoal, 5 minutes on each side, brushing occasionally with marinade. To serve, pour remaining marinade over fish. Serves 4.

GOURMET STUFFED FISH

1 3-lb. carp
⅓ c. chopped fresh mushrooms
½ c. chopped cooked shrimp
⅛ lb. diced, smoked ham
6 water chestnuts, diced
1 T. minced parsley
¼ c. minced scallions
¼ t. pepper
1 t. salt
2 T. ice water
⅓ c. vegetable oil
½ c. cornstarch
1 T. soy sauce
2½ T. sherry
1 T. sugar
2 t. minced gingerroot
½ c. warm water

Have fish split and boned, head removed. Skin fish carefully, reserving skin. Spread skin on flat surface. Chop fish very fine; combine fish, mushrooms, shrimp, ham, water chestnuts, parsley, scallions, salt, pepper, ice water, 1 tablespoon oil, and 1 tablespoon cornstarch. Mix well; spread on one side of fish skin and form into a mound. Cover with the other side of the skin and press edges together; fasten with toothpicks. Dip fish in remaining cornstarch. Heat remaining oil in skillet and brown fish on both sides. Mix together the soy sauce, sherry, sugar, gingerroot and warm water. Pour over fish. Cover and simmer 20 minutes, turning fish once. Serves 6.

PINEAPPLE-PERCH FILLETS

1 lb. fresh or thawed, frozen perch fillets
½ c. pineapple juice
1 T. lime juice
2 t. Worcestershire sauce
½ t. salt
  Pepper
  Lime twists

Cut fish into 4 portions; place in a shallow dish. Combine pineapple juice, lime juice, Worcestershire sauce, salt and a dash of pepper; pour over fish and marinate in refrigerator for 1 hour, turning once. Drain, reserving marinade. Place fillets on a greased rack of broiler pan. Broil 4 inches from heat for 10 minutes or until it flakes easily with a fork, brushing occasionally with the marinade. Heat remaining marinade and spoon over fish before serving. Garnish with lime twists. Serves 4.

ORANGE-RICE STUFFED PERCH

4 fresh pan-dressed perch
½ c. chopped celery
2 T. butter
½ c. uncooked brown rice
¾ c. water
½ t. grated orange peel
½ c. orange juice
1 t. lemon juice
½ t. salt
1 T. chopped parsley
2 T. melted butter
2 T. orange juice

In a small frypan, sauté celery in butter until tender. Stir in rice, water, orange peel, ½ cup orange juice, lemon juice, and salt. Bring to a boil; cover and reduce heat. Simmer until rice is tender, 15 to 20 minutes; stir in parsley. Sprinkle fish cavities with salt; stuff each fish with about ½ cup rice mixture. Skewer closed and place fish in a greased, shallow baking pan. Combine the melted butter and 2 tablespoons orange juice; brush over fish. Bake, uncovered, in a 350° oven about 30 minutes or until fish flakes easily with fork. Baste with butter and orange juice mixture while baking. Serves 4.

SESAME-TOPPED PERCH

1 lb. fresh or thawed, frozen perch fillets
  Salt
½ c. crushed sesame crackers
3 T. melted butter

Cut fish into 3 or 4 portions; place in greased, shallow baking pan. Sprinkle with salt; top with cracker crumbs; drizzle butter over top. Bake in a 325° oven for 25 minutes or until fish flakes easily with a fork. Serves 3 to 4.

PAPRIKA FISH

3 T. vegetable oil
5 green onions, finely chopped
2 tomatoes, chopped
1 clove garlic, minced
2 T. flour
2 t. paprika
  Salt and pepper to taste
2 t. tomato puree, mixed with 1 c. water
  or 1 c. white wine
2 lbs. fish (fresh trout or perch fillets)
¼ c. flour
2 t. salt
4 t. paprika
¼ c. vegetable oil
½ c. sour cream
  Diced cucumber

Heat oil in a covered saucepan. Sauté onions; add garlic and tomatoes. Sprinkle with flour, paprika, salt, and pepper. Add tomato puree mixture. Cover and simmer 20 minutes. Set aside. Roll fish in a mixture of flour, salt, and paprika. Heat 2 tablespoons oil in a skillet; brown the fish. Place fish in saucepan with tomato sauce, cover and simmer 10 minutes. Arrange fish on a platter. Stir the sour cream into the tomato mixture. Heat without boiling; pour sauce over fish. Garnish with cucumber. Serves 4.

Saltwater Fish

HADDOCK A LA RAREBIT

1 c. milk
⅓ c. flour
⅛ t. salt
2 t. prepared mustard
2 c. grated Cheddar cheese
1 T. butter
6 large haddock fillets
Paprika

Heat milk. Sift together flour and salt; add to milk, blending well. Stir in mustard. When slightly thickened, stir in the cheese. When cheese is melted add butter. Lay haddock fillets flat on a buttered oven-proof platter; spread the sauce over and bake in a 375° oven for 30 minutes. Sprinkle with paprika. Serves 6.

CHEDDAR-BAKED HADDOCK

Haddock fillets
Salt and pepper
2 t. chopped onion
3 T. butter
1 c. bread crumbs
¼ c. grated Cheddar cheese
½ c. milk

Season haddock with salt and pepper; place in a greased shallow baking dish. Sauté onion in butter, adding more salt and pepper, bread crumbs and grated cheese. Spread mixture over fillets. Pour milk around fish and bake in a 400° oven about 25 minutes. Allow one-half pound fish per person.

RED SNAPPER IN CAPER SAUCE

4 large red snapper steaks
Dash of salt
1 small onion
1 T. capers
½ c. heavy cream
Dash of pepper
Lemon

Sprinkle fish with salt and let stand for 1 hour; wash salt off and dry fish with a clean cloth. Finely chop onion and capers; spread on steaks; grill slowly 6 to 8 minutes. Carefully put steaks side by side in a buttered dish. Pour cream over steaks; add pepper. Bake in a 425° oven for 15 minutes. Garnish with lemon. Serve with rice. Serves 4.

UNCLE IRVING'S FISH SKILLET

1 lb. red snapper fillets
3 T. vegetable oil
1 onion, chopped
2 T. chopped parsley
1 6-oz. can tomato sauce
½ c. water
½ t. salt
Dash of pepper

Wash fillets and pat dry. Pour oil in skillet. Add onion and sauté over medium heat about 5 minutes. Add remaining ingredients except fish; simmer about 5 minutes. Add fish; cover and simmer 10 minutes or until done, basting once. Serves 4.

DEVILED HALIBUT

¼ c. minced onion
3 T. butter
2 T. flour
1 c. milk
1½ t. salt
1 t. prepared mustard
2 t. Worcestershire sauce
2 t. lemon juice
1 egg, beaten
2 c. flaked, cooked halibut
½ c. bread crumbs

Sauté onion in butter for 5 minutes. Sprinkle with flour and gradually add milk, stirring constantly until mixture reaches boiling point. Add salt, mustard, Worcestershire sauce, lemon juice, egg, and halibut. Mix lightly and divide among 6 buttered baking dishes. Sprinkle with bread crumbs. Bake in a 350° oven for 20 minutes. Serves 6.

HALIBUT STEAK

1 large halibut steak
Melted butter
1 onion, chopped
1 egg yolk, beaten
½ t. salt
¼ t. pepper
1 T. lemon juice
1 T. butter
1 T. flour
¼ c. water

Wash halibut steak and pat dry. Brush bottom of baking pan with melted butter, sprinkle with chopped onion. Place steak on top. Pour egg yolk over fish. Sprinkle with salt and pepper and add lemon juice. Pat on remaining butter. Bake in a 400° oven for 30 minutes. Place fish on a hot platter. Make a sauce in the pan with drippings combined with flour and water. Heat and blend until smooth. Serve hot over fish. One-third pound of steak per person.

CODFISH SOUFFLÉ

1 c. salt codfish
2 c. diced potatoes
1 T. butter
2 eggs, separated
2 T. catsup

Shred the codfish and soak 30 minutes in cold water, or according to directions on the package. Drain. Boil fish with potatoes in salted water until potatoes are tender. Drain and mash the fish-potato mixture; add butter and beat until light. Stir in beaten egg yolks and catsup. Fold in stiffly beaten egg whites, and turn into a greased 1½-quart casserole. Place in a pan of hot water and bake in a 375° oven for 20 minutes. Serves 4 to 6.

BOILED COD

1 2-lb. white codfish
White Sauce (page 22)

Cut codfish into serving portions. Rinse well in cold water. Cover with fresh cold water; refrigerate overnight. An hour before serving, place fish in a large kettle; cover with boiling water and bring to a boil. Simmer 10 minutes. Carefully remove fish to serving platter and pour White Sauce over; serve hot. Serves 4.

MOCK SCALLOPS

2 lb. halibut, ½-inch thick
¾ c. sifted flour
1½ t. salt
¼ t. pepper
¼ t. paprika
1 c. milk
6 T. butter

Cut halibut in ½-inch cubes. Mix together flour, salt, pepper and paprika; dip halibut cubes in milk and then seasoned flour. Sauté halibut "scallops" in butter over low heat until browned. Serves 6 to 8.

CHINESE GINGER SOLE

4 fillets of sole
3 egg yolks
2 T. beer
6 T. cornstarch
½ t. salt
1 c. dried bread crumbs
   Vegetable oil
¼ c. water
4 T. peanut oil
⅓ c. cider vinegar
½ c. chicken stock
¼ c. sugar
2½ T. catsup
1 t. ginger
   Salt and pepper to taste

Wash fillets, pat dry. Beat together egg yolks, beer, 5 tablespoons of the cornstarch, and salt. Dip fish in egg mixture, then in bread crumbs, coating thoroughly. Heat vegetable oil to 375° and fry fillets until browned on both sides. Keep fish hot in oven. Mix remaining cornstarch with water and combine in a saucepan with peanut oil, vinegar, chicken stock, sugar, catsup, ginger, salt and pepper. Cook over low heat, stirring constantly, until thickened. Pour over fish. Serves 4 to 6.

FISH POACHED IN GALLIANO BUTTER

⅔ c. slivered blanched almonds
⅔ c. butter
¼ c. Galliano liqueur
¼ c. lemon juice
1 T. dried dill
   Salt and pepper
2 lbs. fillet of sole

In a large skillet, sauté almonds in butter until lightly toasted, browning butter. Add Galliano, lemon juice and seasonings; add sole. Cover and cook over medium heat 7 to 10 minutes until fish flakes easily with a fork. Spoon Galliano butter over fish often as it cooks. Serves 6.

COLD FISH CURRY

9 fillets of sole
1 c. milk
¼ c. flour
   Salt and pepper
3 T. butter
4 medium onions, peeled and
   thinly sliced
   Vinegar
1½ t. curry powder
1 t. turmeric
1½ T. sugar
½ t. salt

Cover fish with milk and refrigerate for several hours. Drain fish; dry with paper toweling. Dip in flour which has been seasoned with salt and pepper. Sauté fish lightly in butter; place in a glass dish and set aside. In a saucepan cover onions with vinegar. Add seasonings and bring to a boil; cook 4 to 5 minutes. Onions should remain crisp. Pour mixture over fish and refrigerate for 24 hours. Serve cold. Will keep for several days. Serves 3.

FRIED FISH WITH ALMONDS

3 fillets of sole
2 t. grated onion
½ t. ginger
1½ t. salt
1 t. sugar
1 t. cornstarch
2 t. soy sauce
1 t. sherry
1 egg, beaten
¾ c. ground almonds
3 slices ham, cut in 2-inch strips

Cut fillets in half lengthwise and then crosswise, making 4 pieces. Mix together the onion, ginger, salt, sugar, cornstarch, soy sauce, sherry, and egg. Dip fish in the mixture. Dip one side of fish in almonds. Roll each fillet (almond side in) around 1 slice of ham. Deep fry fish until browned. Serves 3.

34

POACHED FISH WITH ALMONDS

½ c. butter
⅔ c. slivered blanched almonds
¼ c. sherry
¼ c. lemon juice
2 T. dill seed
¼ t. salt
¼ t. pepper
1½ lbs. fillet of sole, perch or haddock

Preheat wok to 325°, add butter. Sauté almonds in butter until lightly toasted. Remove almonds and set aside. Put sherry, lemon juice, dill seed, salt, and pepper in wok; stir to blend. Place fillets in sauce, spooning some over top. Reduce heat to 225°, cover and poach 6 to 7 minutes or until fish flakes easily with a fork. After 3 minutes, spoon sauce over fillets and garnish with almonds. Serves 4 to 6.

CREAM OF MULLET

1 lb. mullet fillets
1¼ c. warmed salad oil
¾ c. warm milk
Grated peel and juice of 1 lemon
½ clove garlic, minced
Nutmeg
Pepper

Wash and soak mullet fillets overnight. Drain and rinse. Put fish into a large pot; cover with cold water and bring to a boil. When water boils, mullet is done. Drain immediately. Remove bones but not skin. Work fish and skin alternately with a little oil and milk, adding lemon peel and juice, garlic, nutmeg and pepper. When it is a smooth, creamy paste, reheat, stirring rapidly. Serve with butter-fried triangles of bread. Serves 6.

SWEDISH STYLE BAKED TURBOT

1 lb. frozen turbot, skinless
Salt and pepper to taste
Melted butter
1 16-oz. can tomatoes, drained
½ t. confectioners' sugar
½ onion, sliced in rounds
⅓ c. heavy cream

Dry fish; place in greased baking dish. Season with salt and pepper and brush with melted butter. Add confectioners' sugar to tomatoes and spread over fish; cover with onions. Bake 20 minutes in a 375° oven. Pour cream over fish and bake for an additional 10 minutes; serve at once in same dish. Garnish with thinly sliced dill pickle. Serves 4.

STUFFED SQUID

2 lbs. fresh squid
2½ c. bread crumbs
2 t. parsley
2 T. grated Parmesan cheese
2 T. salad oil
1 medium onion, chopped
Salt and pepper
½ c. salad oil

Clean squid. Combine bread crumbs, parsley, cheese, salad oil, onion, salt and pepper; stuff squid with mixture. Pour oil into shallow baking dish and place stuffed squid carefully in pan. Bake, uncovered, in a 375° oven for 35 minutes. Serves 6.

SWEDISH FISH ROLLS

1 large fillet of sole
Salt
Lemon juice
Mayonnaise
2 or 3 each: carrot sticks, celery sticks, pickle sticks, onion slices
Butter

Salt fish fillet. Rub well with lemon juice and spread mayonnaise on one side. Place the carrot, celery, pickles and onions in the fish; roll jelly-roll fashion. Fasten edges with toothpicks. Spread butter over top. In an oven-proof glass baking dish, bake in a 200° oven for 1½ to 2 hours. Serves 4.

SWEET-SOUR FISH

1 2-lb. sea bass (1 large or 3 small-
   mouthed bass)
   Gingerroot slices
1 T. dry sherry
½ c. sugar
⅓ c. cider vinegar
1 T. soy sauce
¼ t. gingerroot juice
2 T. cornstarch
1 clove garlic, crushed

Rinse fish in cold water and drain. Slash each fish crosswise on each side along backbone in meaty part, making three equal diagonal cuts. Bring enough water to boil in a large, shallow pan to completely cover fish. Gently lower fish into water; add sherry and ginger slices. Cover tightly and remove at once from heat. Let stand 15 to 20 minutes; fish will be cooked. Meanwhile, combine remaining ingredients in a small saucepan and cook, stirring, until thickened. Discard garlic. Carefully remove fish to serving platter and pour on hot sauce. Serves 2.

JAPANESE BOILED BASS

2 qts. water
1½ T. lemon juice
2 lbs. cleaned fresh sea bass, cut in
   3-inch squares
   Salt and pepper
2 T. peanut oil
¼ c. chopped green onion
½ c. teriyaki sauce, heated

In Dutch oven, bring water to a rolling boil. Add lemon juice and fish; return to boil. Turn off heat, cover, and let fish stand in hot water 15 to 20 minutes, depending upon thickness of fish. Drain, place on platter and season with salt and pepper. Pour peanut oil over fish, sprinkle with green onion and teriyaki sauce. Serve fish immediately with remaining sauce. Serves 4.

LEMON-BARBECUED SWORDFISH STEAKS

3 lbs. of swordfish steaks,
   sliced 1 inch thick
¾ c. lemon juice
¾ c. salad oil
2 T. prepared horseradish
1 T. grated lemon peel
1½ t. salt
½ t. basil
½ t. oregano
½ t. pepper
   Lemon quarters

Place swordfish steaks in shallow dish. Blend remaining ingredients and pour over fish. Chill, covered, several hours or overnight. Drain fish, reserving marinade and grill over slow to medium coals, 6 to 8 minutes on each side, basting frequently with marinade. Garnish with lemon quarters. Serves 8.

SWORDFISH BAKE

2 lbs. quartered fresh swordfish steaks
¼ c. lime juice
   Pepper to taste
3 medium tomatoes, halved horizontally
4 medium bananas, peeled
½ c. melted butter
⅓ c. dried bread crumbs
1 t. parsley
½ t. dried savory

Place fish in large baking dish and sprinkle with half of the lime juice. Season with pepper. Brush tomato halves with melted butter. Combine crumbs, parsley, and savory; spoon evenly over tomato halves. Arrange tomatoes and bananas around fish. Lightly brush fish, bananas, and tomatoes with butter. Bake in a 375° oven for 7 minutes. Turn fish and bananas; sprinkle fish lightly with remaining lime juice. Brush fish and bananas with butter and bake 7 minutes longer, or until fish flakes easily with a fork. Serves 4.

Salmon and Tuna

TEMPURA CANNED SALMON

1 7¾-oz. can pink salmon; drain, save juice
¼ c. juice from salmon
1 egg
½ c. flour
1 t. baking powder

In a mixing bowl, add egg to salmon. Sift in enough flour to make a thick, sticky paste. Mix together baking powder and salmon juice. Stir quickly into salmon mixture. Drop by teaspoonfuls into hot oil. Brown quickly; drain. Serves 2.

CHEESE-SALMON LOAF

1 1-lb. can salmon, flaked
1½ c. grated American cheese
1 egg, beaten
½ c. light cream
½ t. salt
1 c. bread crumbs
3 T. melted butter
1 T. lemon juice
¼ t. pepper
   Buttered bread crumbs
   Celery Sauce (page 22)

Combine all ingredients except buttered bread crumbs. Shape into a loaf and put in a buttered loaf pan. Sprinkle with crumbs. Bake in a 350° oven for 30 minutes. Serve hot or cold with Celery Sauce. Serves 6.

BAKED STUFFED SALMON OR TROUT

5 to 6 lb. salmon or trout, cleaned with head and tail intact
   Salt and pepper
   Juice from ½ lemon
½ c. butter
2 large onions, sliced ¼-inch thick
2 green peppers cut into thin strips
3 cloves garlic, minced
1 1-lb. 14-oz. can solid pack tomatoes, chopped
1 t. oregano
1 t. basil
1 large bay leaf
½ c. white wine
2 T. butter

Rinse fish and pat dry; sprinkle skin and cavities with salt, pepper, and lemon juice. Melt ½ cup butter in skillet and sauté onions, pepper strips and minced garlic until onion is softened. Add tomatoes, oregano, basil, bay leaf, and salt and pepper to taste; add wine. Bring to a rapid boil, remove from heat and allow to cool slightly. Stuff salmon with the tomato mixture and skewer the opening. Pour any leftover mixture over the salmon and dot with 2 tablespoons butter. Bake in a 425° oven for 25 minutes or until fish flakes easily when tested with a fork. Baste fish every 5 minutes while baking. Serves 6.

Pictured opposite:
Cheese-Salmon Loaf
Celery Sauce, p. 22

SATURDAY SALMON SUPPER

3 T. chopped onion
⅓ c. chopped green pepper
3 T. butter
1 t. salt
¼ c. flour
1 10½-oz. can cream of celery or
  mushroom soup
1½ c. milk
1 7-oz. can salmon, drained
1 c. cooked peas
1 T. lemon juice
  Biscuit Dough (page 20)

Sauté onion and pepper in butter until onion
is golden; blend in salt and flour. Gradually
stir in soup and milk. Boil for 1 minute. Add
salmon, peas and lemon juice. Pour into an
11½ x 7½ x 1½-inch baking dish. Drop
Biscuit Dough by teaspoonfuls over mixture in dish. Bake in a 450° oven for 10 to 12
minutes or until biscuits are done. Serves 4.

SALMON SOUFFLÉ
WITH YELLOW SAUCE

1 c. salmon
¼ t. salt
¼ t. pepper
½ c. milk
½ c. bread crumbs
4 eggs, separated
  Yellow Sauce (page 22)

Remove all bones from salmon. Chop fine
and add seasonings. Heat milk and bread
crumbs together for 5 minutes; add egg
yolks and salmon. Beat egg whites stiff and
fold into salmon mixture. Turn into a buttered baking dish. Set dish in pan of hot
water. Bake in a 350° oven until firm. Serve
with Yellow Sauce. Serves 2 to 4.

FISHERMAN STYLE POTATOES
STUFFED WITH SALMON

6 medium potatoes
⅓ c. milk
1 egg, beaten
1 t. salt
¼ t. paprika
1 T. lemon juice
2 T. butter
1½ c. flaked salmon
⅓ c. minced onion
  Buttered bread crumbs

Bake potatoes; remove from oven and split
lengthwise into halves. Scoop out potatoes;
mash and add milk, egg, salt, paprika, and
lemon juice; beat until light and fluffy. Melt
butter in saucepan. Sauté salmon and onion
until onion is tender. Fold into mashed
potato. Refill potato shells; sprinkle with
buttered bread crumbs and bake in a 350°
oven for 25 minutes. Serves 6.

COLD SALMON WITH
REMOULADE SAUCE

3 hard-boiled eggs, chopped
1 egg yolk, beaten
1 T. vinegar
3 T. olive oil
1 t. prepared brown mustard
½ t. sugar
  Juice of ½ lemon
  Salt and pepper
1 t. horseradish
2 lb. salmon steak
4 c. white wine
8 peppercorns
1 bay leaf

Mix hard-boiled eggs, egg yolk, vinegar,
olive oil, mustard, sugar, lemon juice, salt,
pepper and horseradish. Wipe and place
salmon steak in large frying pan. Pour wine
over; add peppercorns and bay leaf. Poach
20 to 30 minutes. Drain; refrigerate. Serve
with sauce. Serves 4.

MARINATED SALMON

6 slices of salmon
3 Bermuda onions, sliced
3 c. water
2 t. salt
½ c. lemon juice
½ c. white vinegar
1 t. pickling spice
1 bay leaf
¼ t. whole peppercorns

Combine salmon, onions, water, and salt in a Dutch oven. Bring to a boil and simmer 25 minutes. Carefully transfer salmon to a platter. Add lemon juice, vinegar, pickling spice, bay leaf and peppercorns to the fish stock. Bring to a boil and cook 2 minutes. Pour over fish and chill 24 hours before serving. Drain and serve cold. Serves 6 to 8.

SALMON LOAF AND SAUCE

1 1-lb. can salmon (remove bones)
1 egg, beaten
3¼ T. milk
1 T. butter
Salt and pepper to taste
⅓ c. cracker crumbs
Buttered cracker crumbs
½ c. heavy cream, whipped
Salt and paprika to taste
2 T. vinegar
1 medium cucumber, pared, chopped and drained
1 t. grated onion

Mix together first six ingredients; form into a loaf in baking pan; cover with buttered cracker crumbs. Bake in a 350° oven for 30 minutes until light brown. To make sauce, add salt and paprika to whipped cream; gradually add vinegar, cucumber and onion. Serves 4 to 6.

SCRAMBLED EGGS WITH FISH

1 T. melted butter
1 c. fish (use canned tuna, salmon or crab)
6 eggs, beaten
1 T. water
Salt and pepper to taste
2 T. butter
4 slices toast
Bacon slices

Heat butter in saucepan. Drain fish, remove skin and bones; break fish into small pieces. Sauté in butter. With a fork beat together eggs, water, pepper and salt; add the butter cut into small pieces. Pour over fish and stir slowly with a wooden spoon, scraping the sides and bottom of the pan. When eggs are cooked, but still creamy, serve on buttered toast with bacon slices. Serves 4.

TUNA-GHETTI A LA PARMESAN

¼ c. butter
1 c. minced onion
¼ t. garlic powder
1½ t. salt
¼ t. pepper
1 t. oregano
¼ c. minced parsley
1 1-lb. can tomatoes
1 8-oz. can tomato sauce
½ c. grated Parmesan cheese
1 9-oz. can tuna
3 T. flour
1 1-lb. pkg. spaghetti

In a 3-quart pot, melt butter; add onion and sauté until tender. Remove from heat. Stir in garlic powder, salt, pepper, oregano, and parsley. Add tomatoes, tomato sauce, cheese and tuna broken into large pieces. Stir; simmer for 30 minutes. Mix a few spoonfuls of tomato mixture with flour, return to saucepan. Simmer a few minutes more. Cook spaghetti according to package directions. Pour tomato-tuna mixture over spaghetti. Serves 6 to 8.

TUNA WITH ASPARAGUS AND ALMONDS

2 T. butter
2 T. flour
1 c. milk *or* ½ c. white wine and
   ½ c. water
1 egg yolk
½ c. cream
1 t. lemon juice
¼ t. salt
¼ t. pepper
¼ t. mace
1 6½-oz. can tuna, salmon or crab
4 T. shredded almonds
15 to 20 cooked asparagus spears
   Chopped almonds
   Butter
2 t. chopped parsley
   Pepper

Melt butter; stir in flour. Slowly add milk, stirring with a wire whisk. Simmer 5 minutes. Remove from heat. Mix egg yolk with cream and lemon juice. Stir into sauce and add seasonings. Add drained fish, broken into pieces. Add shredded almonds. Arrange asparagus in a buttered oven-proof dish; cover with fish mixture. Sprinkle with chopped almonds, dot with butter and bake in a 350° oven for 30 minutes. Garnish with parsley and pepper. Serves 6.

TUNA-STUFFED POTATOES

4 large, hot, baked potatoes
2 T. butter
½ 7-oz. can tuna, drained and flaked
   (reserve oil)
½ c. scalded milk
½ T. salt
½ t. pepper
1 T. minced onion

Slice tops from baked potatoes lengthwise. Scoop out potato and mash. Beat in butter, oil from tuna, hot milk, seasoning, onion and flaked tuna. Put mixture in potato shells, place in shallow baking dish and bake in a 450° oven for 10 minutes or until light brown. Serves 4.

TUNA BAKED IN SHELLS

1½ T. butter
1 T. flour
1 c. milk
½ t. salt
¼ t. pepper
½ t. paprika
1 7-oz. can tuna, flaked
½ c. bread crumbs
2 hard-boiled eggs, chopped
1 T. lemon juice
1 t. Worcestershire sauce
4 T. grated cheese
   Baking shells

Melt butter, blend in flour; add milk and seasonings and simmer until thickened, stirring constantly. Add tuna, bread crumbs, eggs, lemon juice and Worcestershire sauce. Fill baking shells and sprinkle with additional crumbs and grated cheese. Bake in a 350° oven for 30 minutes. Serves 4.

TUNA QUICHE

1 9-inch pie shell
½ lb. bacon
1 small onion, sliced
¼ lb. Swiss cheese, grated
1 6½-oz. can tuna
3 eggs, slightly beaten
1¼ c. light cream
½ t. salt
¼ t. monosodium glutamate
   Dash of hot sauce
   Nutmeg

Fry bacon until crisp; drain and crumble. Save bacon drippings. Fry onion in bacon drippings until tender. Place cheese in pie shell; top with bacon, onion and tuna. Mix eggs with cream, salt, monosodium glutamate and hot sauce; pour over tuna mixture and sprinkle with nutmeg. Bake in a 425° oven 15 minutes. Reduce temperature to 325° and bake 25 to 30 minutes longer, or until knife inserted in center comes out clean. Serves 4 to 6.

CREAMY TUNA

6 slices bacon, cut in 1-inch pieces
1 medium onion, sliced in rounds
2 green onions, chopped
1 10½-oz. can cream of mushroom soup
½ c. evaporated milk
1 4-oz. can button mushrooms and liquid
1 7-oz. can tuna, flaked
2 T. minced parsley
  Sauce and gravy flour
  Dash of Tabasco sauce

Fry bacon pieces until done, but not crisp; remove and set aside. Pour off fat, reserving 1 tablespoon; sauté onion. Combine soup, milk, and mushroom liquid; add to fat. Stir in fried bacon, button mushrooms, flaked tuna and parsley, stirring constantly. If mixture is too thin, sift in flour and stir. Add Tabasco sauce, if desired. Serve hot over rice or noodles. Serves 2.

Note: For a richer texture, add undiluted evaporated milk.

TUNA-RICE PATTIES IN TOMATO SAUCE

1 9-oz. can tuna
2 c. steamed rice
1 egg, slightly beaten
1 T. chopped onion
2 T. chopped parsley
1 T. flour
1 t. salt
2 T. butter
2 T. grated onion
2 T. chopped green pepper
1 10½-oz. can tomato soup
  Few drops of Tabasco

Blend tuna and rice. Combine egg, chopped onion, parsley, flour and salt, mixing well. Add to tuna mixture. Form in small flat cakes and fry in oil until golden brown. Sauté grated onion and green pepper in butter. Add tomato soup and Tabasco. Serve over Tuna-Rice Patties. Serves 4 to 6.

BOYCOTT CASSEROLE

1 6-oz. pkg. noodles, cooked
1 12½-oz. can tuna
3 hard-boiled eggs
½ c. peas
½ c. carrots, diced
1 T. parsley
1 T. minced onion
2 T. mayonnaise
1 T. mustard
¼ c. Parmesan cheese
  Butter
  Parsley

Combine all ingredients except butter and parsley; bake in a 350° oven for 1 hour. Pat with butter and garnish with parsley. Serves 4 to 5.

EASY TUNA CASSEROLE

1 small avocado, peeled and diced
½ c. chopped watercress
  Salt to taste
¼ c. grated onion
1 12½-oz. can tuna
1 10½-oz. can cream of chicken soup
2 pieces crisp bacon, crumbled
  Crushed potato chips

Arrange avocado in casserole dish. Sprinkle with watercress, salt and onion. Heat soup, add tuna and bacon. Pour into casserole. Garnish with crushed potato chips. Bake in a 450° oven for 10 minutes. Serves 2.

TUNA-BROCCOLI CASSEROLE

1 pkg. frozen, chopped broccoli
1 7-oz. can tuna, drained and broken
½ c. milk
1 10½-oz. can cream of mushroom soup
¼ t. salt
  Biscuit Dough (page 20)

Steam broccoli according to package directions until almost tender. Place in a greased 9 x 9 x 2-inch pan. Cover with tuna. Combine soup, milk, and salt and pour over top. Make Biscuit Dough. Drop by teaspoonfuls over mixture in pan. Bake in a 450° oven for 15 minutes. Serves 6.

Lobster, Crab, and Shrimp

LOBSTER WITH COGNAC

1 large lobster
Butter
Minced shallot
Minced parsley
Salt and pepper
½ c. cognac
3 T. heavy cream

Split lobster in half lengthwise. Spread surfaces with butter mixed with shallot and parsley; season with salt and pepper. Bake in a 425° oven 15 minutes. Remove from oven; pour warmed cognac over and flame. Pour cream over and return to oven briefly to blend pan juices. Serves 2.

BROILED LOBSTER TAILS

6 small frozen lobster tails
Melted butter
Salt and pepper to taste

Thaw lobster. With a kitchen scissors, cut along the inner edges of the soft undershell, clipping off fins along the outer edges. Peel back and discard the soft undershell. Bend back the overshell to crack some of the joints and prevent curling. Place lobster tail, meat side up, on a greased broiler rack 2 inches from heat. Brush meat with melted butter; sprinkle with salt and pepper. Broil 15 to 20 minutes or until browned. Turn; broil 5 to 10 minutes. Serve with melted butter. Serves 3.

LOBSTER NEWBURG

2 c. cooked lobster, cut up
¼ c. butter
½ t. salt
Dash of cayenne
Dash of nutmeg
½ c. cream
2 egg yolks
2 T. sherry

Heat lobster by frying slowly in butter for 3 minutes. Add seasonings and heat 1 minute. Add cream and slightly beaten egg yolks; simmer 3 minutes more. Add sherry and serve. Serves 2 to 4.

GERMAN LOBSTER IN BEER

1 lobster
1 pt. light beer
Butter
3 shallots, chopped
½ t. caraway seed
¼ t. pepper
1 T. flour
1 T. cold water

Split lobster for broiling. Place lobster in large skillet with beer; cover. Bring to a boil and boil for 3 minutes. Remove lobster from beer and dot with butter; broil 5 minutes. Reduce beer to 2 cups; add shallots, caraway seeds and pepper; simmer 5 minutes. Add flour mixed with 1 tablespoon cold water. Strain sauce and serve over lobster. Serve with hot potato salad. Serves 1.

LOBSTER WITH GALLIANO CRUMBS

6 c. fresh bread crumbs
2½ c. chopped fresh parsley
¾ c. Galliano liqueur
¾ c. melted butter
⅓ c. lemon juice
2 T. salt
1½ t. pepper
1 T. oregano leaves
6 live lobsters

Combine bread crumbs, parsley, Galliano, butter, lemon juice, and seasonings; set aside. Plunge the lobsters into a large pot of boiling water and boil 5 minutes. Remove at once and place on a firm surface. Split each lobster open and remove dark vein and small sac below the head. Stuff lobsters with crumb mixture and broil 5 minutes or until stuffing is browned and lobsters are cooked. Serves 6.

LOBSTER ORIENTAL

2 lbs. lobster
1 8-oz. can button mushrooms
1 T. salad oil
1 clove garlic
½ c. diced celery
½ c. diced bamboo shoots
½ c. diced water chestnuts
1 c. Chinese pea pods
2 t. cornstarch
½ t. sugar
½ t. salt
1 t. soy sauce
½ c. chicken broth
¾ c. cashew nuts

Shell lobster and cut into 1-inch pieces. Drain mushrooms and cut into quarters. Heat oil in skillet; sauté garlic and remove. Sauté lobster 30 seconds. Add mushrooms, celery, bamboo shoots, water chestnuts, and pea pods. Stir fry 30 seconds. Mix cornstarch with sugar, salt, soy sauce, and broth; stir into vegetable mixture. Simmer, stirring constantly, until sauce thickens; quickly stir in cashews. Serve immediately. Serves 6.

LOBSTER CASSEROLE

2 5-oz. cans of lobster
½ c. mayonnaise
1 c. diced onion
1 c. diced celery
3 c. milk
4 eggs, slightly beaten
Dash of pepper
8 slices white bread with crusts removed
1 10½-oz. can mushroom soup, undiluted
½ c. grated Monterey Jack cheese
Paprika
Rice

Mix lobster, mayonnaise, onion, celery, milk, eggs and pepper; set aside. Grease a large casserole, put 4 slices bread in casserole. Spread ½ mixture over bread; add remaining bread and mixture; refrigerate overnight. Bake in a 350° oven for 15 minutes. Remove; spread soup on top. Add cheese and sprinkle with paprika. Bake in a 350° oven uncovered for 1 hour. Serve with rice. Serves 4.

LOBSTER SOUTH PACIFIC

1 c. coarsely chopped mango, skinned
1 c. coarsely chopped papaya, skinned
2¼ c. coarsely chopped and cooked, fresh lobster
1 c. thinly sliced celery
¼ c. heavy cream
½ t. grated lemon rind
2 t. lemon juice
2 t. soy sauce
1 t. grated onion
¼ t. ginger
1 t. honey
Pepper to taste
Cold lettuce leaves
½ bunch watercress, stems removed
2 T. toasted slivered almonds

Combine fruit, lobster, and celery in a large wooden salad bowl; toss. Combine cream, lemon rind and juice, soy sauce, onion, ginger, honey, and pepper; stir until smooth. Pour over lobster and fruit and toss lightly; chill thoroughly. Serve on lettuce. Garnish with watercress and almonds. Serves 4.

ELEGANT BROILED LOBSTER

1 T. salt per 4 cups of water
3 whole fresh lobsters
6 T. soy sauce
1 T. sherry
½ t. paprika
½ c. melted butter

In a very large pot, add salt to enough water to cover lobsters. Bring to a boil. Plunge lobsters in water; boil for 20 minutes. Cool and remove legs and shell. Split lobsters lengthwise, cutting halfway through. Combine soy sauce and sherry; pour over lobsters. Broil lobsters 4 inches from heat, basting with sauce several times until lobsters flake easily with a fork. When lobsters are done, sprinkle with paprika and spoon some of the melted butter on top. Serve with remaining butter. Serves 6.

SLIMMER CRAB CAKES

1 t. prepared mustard
2 T. salad dressing
1 egg
1 lb. crab meat
Salt and pepper
¼ t. dry mustard
½ c. cracker meal
Parsley
Vegetable oil

Mix together prepared mustard, salad dressing, and egg; add remaining ingredients. Mix lightly so as not to break up the crab meat. Form into cakes; fry in small amount of oil until brown; turn and brown on other side. These may also be broiled. Serves 4.

KING CRAB AU GRATIN

1½ lbs. king crab meat, cooked
¼ lb. butter
¼ c. flour
1 c. milk
1 c. light cream
½ c. white wine
1 c. grated sharp Cheddar cheese
1 T. salt
¼ t. paprika
1 4½-oz. can sliced mushrooms
2 T. grated onion
⅓ c. dry bread crumbs

Melt butter and stir in flour; gradually stir in milk, cream, and wine. Simmer over low heat, stirring constantly. Add cheese, salt, paprika, mushrooms, and onion; stir until cheese is melted. Fold in chunks of crab. Pour into a well-greased, 2-quart casserole; top with bread crumbs. Bake in a 400° oven 10 to 12 minutes. Serves 4.

CRAB CASSEROLE I

3 T. butter
3 T. flour
Salt, pepper, paprika to taste
2 c. milk
1 7½-oz. can crab meat, drained and cut into 1-inch pieces
1 c. cooked peas
5 hard-boiled eggs, sliced
Juice of ½ lemon
Bread crumbs
Butter
Lemon slices

Melt butter; blend in flour, salt, pepper and paprika; add milk slowly, stirring until smooth; add crab, peas, 4 sliced hard-boiled eggs and lemon juice. Place mixture in a casserole; sprinkle with bread crumbs and dabs of butter. Bake in a 350° oven until top browns and mixture is heated. Garnish with rest of egg slices and lemon slices. Serves 4 to 6.

CRAB MEAT AND PORK

2½ T. vegetable oil
¼ lb. ground pork
2 eggs, beaten
2 T. soy sauce
1 T. sherry
1 t. salt
½ t. sugar
2 T. water
1 lb. crab meat
3 green onions, chopped

Heat oil in a skillet; sauté pork for 5 minutes. Stir in eggs and quickly add soy sauce, sherry, salt, sugar, water, and crab meat. Mix well and simmer over low heat for 4 minutes. Sprinkle with chopped green onion. Serves 4 to 6.

CRAB BISQUE

1 10½-oz. can cream of mushroom soup
1 10½-oz. can cream of asparagus soup
1 7½-oz. can crab meat, drained, coarse parts removed
1⅛ c. evaporated milk
1 c. light cream
⅓ c. dry sherry

Mix all ingredients together; heat. Serve on hot rice or toast. Serves 2.

SEAFOOD PARISIENNE

2 9-oz. pkgs. frozen artichoke hearts
2 c. uncooked rice
1½ lb. cooked shrimp, lobster, or crab meat
2 10½-oz. cans Cheddar cheese soup
2⅔ c. water
1 T. lemon juice
½ t. dill
½ t. salt
¼ t. garlic powder
Lemon wedges

Cook artichoke hearts as directed on package; drain and place in a 3-quart casserole. Stir in rice and shrimp. Mix remaining ingredients, except lemon wedges; pour into casserole. Cover and bake in a 400° oven for 35 minutes; stir before serving. Serve with lemon wedges. Serves 8.

LOVELY CRAB

8 slices white bread, crusts removed
8 thin slices mild cheese
1 7½-oz. can crab meat, drained
3 eggs, beaten
¼ t. Worcestershire sauce
  Dash of paprika, onion salt and monosodium glutamate
  Salt and pepper to taste
1½ c. milk
1 T. sherry

Line bottom of a casserole dish with half of the white bread; cover with slices of mild cheese. Add crab, topped by another layer of bread. Mix remaining ingredients together and pour over bread mixture. Refrigerate 5 hours. Place casserole in a pan of hot water; bake in a 350° oven for 50 minutes. Remove cover the last 10 minutes. Serves 4.

CRAB MEAT A LA MARINARA

⅛ t. cayenne
⅛ t. onion powder
¼ t. garlic powder
¾ t. basil
1¼ t. oregano
4 whole black peppercorns
2½ t. salt
¼ t. sugar
¼ c. olive oil
1 T. parsley flakes
8 medium tomatoes
2 7½-oz. cans crab meat
  Cooked spaghetti or rice

Combine first 10 ingredients; peel tomatoes, dice and add to seasonings. Simmer, uncovered, 20 minutes or until thick. Add crab and simmer 5 minutes or until hot. Serve over well-drained cooked spaghetti or rice. Serves 6.

CRAB AND AVOCADO CASSEROLE

1 large avocado, peeled and sliced
3 T. lime juice
1 6-oz. can crab meat, drained
  Salt and pepper
½ 10½-oz. can mushroom soup
1 T. milk
  Buttered bread crumbs

Sprinkle avocado with lime juice. Layer avocado and crab, lightly sprinkling each layer with salt and pepper. Combine mushroom soup with milk; pour over crab. Top with buttered bread crumbs. Heat in a 350° oven for 20 minutes. Serves 2.

FANCY CRAB CASSEROLE

2½ c. cooked rice
1 c. mayonnaise
½ c. milk
1 c. tomato juice
½ c. chopped green onion
½ c. chopped green pepper
½ c. sliced, blanched almonds
2 7½-oz. cans crab meat, drained

Combine all ingredients, mixing well. Place in a buttered casserole. (Mixture will be thin.) Bake, uncovered, in a 350° oven for 45 minutes. Serves 6.

CRAB CASSEROLE II

1½ pkgs. wide noodles
2 7½-oz. cans crab meat
1 5-oz. can lobster
1 10½-oz. can mushroom soup
½ c. water
1¼ c. grated sharp Cheddar cheese
½ of medium Bermuda onion, minced
  Salt and pepper to taste
  English muffins

Cook noodles. Combine remaining ingredients except English muffins; stir in noodles. Pour into a buttered 2-quart casserole. Bake in a 350° oven for 30 minutes. Serve with English muffins. Serves 6 to 8.

CRAB BOATS

2 T. butter
⅓ c. sliced button mushrooms
¾ c. chopped celery
1 lb. cooked crab meat
¾ c. sliced water chestnuts
3 ripe avocados
  Lemon juice
1 c. Quick Hollandaise Sauce (page 21)
3 T. butter
1 c. light cream
1 T. Dijon mustard
1 t. Worcestershire sauce
½ t. sugar
3 drops Tabasco
  Juice of ½ lime
  Salt to taste
½ c. blanched toasted almonds
1 T. brandy
2 T. chopped parsley
  Slivered almonds

Heat 2 tablespoons of butter in a skillet; add mushrooms and celery; sauté for 5 minutes, stirring constantly. Add crab and water chestnuts. Stir together, then cover and simmer. Halve avocados and rub surface with lemon juice. Put avocados in a shallow dish filled with ½-inch of hot water. Bake in a 400° oven for 10 minutes. Make Quick Hollandaise Sauce; set aside. In a saucepan, melt 3 tablespoons butter; add cream, mustard, Worcestershire sauce, sugar and Tabasco; add the hollandaise sauce. Heat, stirring constantly. Stir in lime juice and salt. Add crab mixture and almonds. Stir in brandy and parsley. Remove avocados to a serving dish and fill with hot crab mixture. Top with slivered almonds. Serves 6.

Pictured opposite: Crab Casserole II

SWEET AND SOUR SHRIMP

¼ c. brown sugar
2 T. cornstarch
½ t. salt
¼ c. vinegar
1 T. soy sauce
¼ t. ginger
2½ c. canned pineapple chunks and syrup
1 green pepper, diced
2 small onions, cut in rings
1 lb. cooked shrimp, deveined
Rice

In a saucepan combine sugar, cornstarch and salt; mix until smooth. Add vinegar, soy sauce, ginger and syrup drained from the pineapple. Simmer, stirring constantly, until slightly thickened. Add green pepper, onion, and pineapple chunks; simmer 2 minutes. Add shrimp; bring to a boil, stirring constantly. Serve immediately over hot rice. Serves 3 to 4.

SHRIMP CREOLE

1½ c. chopped onion
1 c. chopped celery
2 medium green peppers, finely chopped
2 cloves garlic, minced
¼ c. butter or margarine
1 15-oz. can tomato sauce
1 c. water
1½ t. salt
⅛ t. cayenne
2 bay leaves, crushed
2 t. snipped parsley
14 to 16-oz. fresh cleaned shrimp
3 c. hot cooked rice

Sauté onion, celery, green pepper, and garlic in butter until onion is tender. Remove from heat and stir in tomato sauce, water, and seasonings. Simmer, uncovered, for 10 minutes, adding water if needed. Stir in shrimp and heat to boiling; cover and simmer over medium heat 10 to 20 minutes or until shrimp are pink and tender. Serve over hot rice. Serves 6.

SESAME-SHRIMP AND ASPARAGUS

1 lb. fresh asparagus
1 lb. shrimp, shelled and deveined
1 medium onion, sliced
¼ c. salad oil
2 T. sesame seeds, toasted
1 T. soy sauce
1 t. salt

Prepare asparagus, cut in 2-inch pieces and set aside. In large skillet fry shrimp, asparagus and onions in hot oil over medium-high heat; stir-fry until shrimp are pink and vegetables are tender-crisp. Stir in sesame seeds, soy sauce and salt until mixed. Serves 4.

SPECIAL SEAFOOD CASSEROLE

1 lb. cooked shrimp
4 T. butter
½ c. minced onion
½ c. minced green pepper
1 10½-oz. can cream of mushroom soup
¾ c. milk
1 2-oz. can chopped mushrooms
3 c. cooked rice
1 6½-oz. can crab meat, flaked
1 c. buttered bread crumbs
½ c. grated Cheddar cheese

Set aside 10 whole shrimp. Cut remaining shrimp in half and set aside. Melt butter and sauté onion and green pepper until tender. Add soup, milk, and mushrooms with liquid; simmer 10 minutes. Fold in rice. Set aside about 1½ cups soup mixture. To remaining soup mixture, add cut shrimp and crab meat. Pour in a 2-quart greased casserole. Pour remaining soup mixture over; sprinkle with bread crumbs and grated cheese. Split remaining shrimp lengthwise and place on top of casserole. Bake in a 350° oven for 30 minutes. Serves 8.

SHERRIED SHRIMP

1 4½-oz. can (medium) shrimp, deveined and minced
¼ c. minced parsley
2 hard-boiled eggs, minced
2 t. melted butter
  Salt and pepper
¼ c. cream
½ c. sherry
  Hot croutons or waffles

In a saucepan mix all ingredients except sherry and croutons. Simmer 5 minutes and add sherry. Serve on hot croutons or waffles. Serves 2.

TERIYAKI SHRIMP

2 lbs. fresh shrimp
½ c. soy sauce
¼ c. sugar
1 clove garlic, crushed
1 small piece ginger, crushed
¼ t. monosodium glutamate

Wash shrimp and remove legs. Butterfly by lengthwise cutting back of each shrimp through the shell; flatten and remove vein. In a shallow dish combine remaining ingredients. Place shrimp, shell side up in soy sauce mixture. Marinate 45 minutes or longer. Place on rack, shell side down. Broil 3 inches from heat for 3 to 4 minutes. Turn and broil 2 minutes longer. Serves 4.

SHRIMP TEMPURA

¾ c. flour
¼ c. water
1 egg
½ t. salt
1½ t. sugar
  Pinch of monosodium glutamate
6 shrimp, finely chopped
1 8-oz. can water chestnuts, finely chopped
2 green onions, finely chopped

Mix together flour, water, egg, salt, sugar and monosodium glutamate. Add shrimp, water chestnuts and green onion. Drop by teaspoonfuls into hot oil and fry. Serves 2.

SHRIMP DIJON

1 large clove garlic, mashed
¾ c. butter, softened
1 t. salt
⅛ t. tarragon
⅛ t. marjoram
  Dash of Tabasco
1 c. fine bread crumbs
½ c. sherry
3 lbs. cooked shrimp
¼ c. chopped parsley

Combine garlic, butter, salt, tarragon, marjoram, and Tabasco; cream until well blended. Add bread crumbs and sherry. In a 2-quart buttered baking dish, place alternate layers of shrimp and bread crumb mixture, sprinkling chopped parsley over each layer. Bake in a 400° oven for 20 to 25 minutes. Serves 6.

SHRIMP CURRY ORIENTAL

1 lb. medium shrimp
1 slice gingerroot, crushed
1 clove garlic, crushed
1 T. vegetable oil
1 t. soy sauce
¼ t. sesame oil
1 T. curry
2 t. salt
¼ t. monosodium glutamate
½ t. sugar
1 onion, cubed
1 c. frozen peas
1 stalk celery, cut in ½-inch lengths
1 carrot, cubed
⅓ c. evaporated milk
1 T. cornstarch
2 stalks green onion, cut in ½-inch slices
  Rice

Shell and clean shrimp; cut each in half. Brown gingerroot and garlic in vegetable oil; add next six ingredients and simmer. Add onion, peas, celery, and carrot. Heat 5 minutes. Add shrimp and milk. Simmer about 6 minutes. Add cornstarch, blending well; heat, stirring constantly until thickened. Add green onions. Serve with rice. Serves 4.

QUICK SEAFOOD NEWBURG

2 envelopes sherry wine sauce mix
½ lb. frozen shrimp, thawed
½ lb. frozen crab meat, thawed
  Dash of salt and pepper
2 T. Worcestershire sauce
  Rice
1 T. finely chopped parsley
  Paprika
2 t. sherry

Prepare wine sauce as directed on envelope; add shrimp and crab meat and stir gently until well heated. Add salt and pepper; add Worcestershire sauce a little at a time. Serve over rice. Garnish with finely chopped parsley and paprika. Just before serving, sprinkle with sherry. Serves 3 to 4.

PRAWNS IN ENVELOPES

8 6-inch squares waxed paper
4 prawns
  Salt and pepper
1 t. sherry
  Monosodium glutamate
  Peanut oil
8 slices gingerroot
8 slices green onion
8 Chinese pea pods

Shell and clean prawns. Cut each prawn in half. Add salt, pepper, sherry and monosodium glutamate; mix well. Rub each square of waxed paper with oil. Place one slice prawn, one slice gingerroot, 1 slice onion and 1 Chinese pea pod on each piece of paper. Make a triangle with the paper by folding the bottom corner nearest you over the ingredients to about 1-inch from the opposite top corner. Fold the right corner over toward the left and crease the edge. Then fold the left corner toward the right side, and crease the edge. Take the bottom of the packet, fold toward the top point or flap. Tuck flap in-between the two folded sides to secure. Deep fry flap side down until light brown in color. Remove waxed paper before eating. Serves 2.

SHRIMP MEUNIERE

2 cloves garlic, diced
½ t. salt
¼ c. melted butter
¼ c. olive oil
2 lbs. shrimp, shelled and deveined
2 T. lemon juice
1 T. chopped parsley

In large skillet crush garlic with the salt to a paste. Add butter and oil; heat. Add shrimp and fry gently, stirring often for 5 to 10 minutes or until done. Remove from heat; add lemon juice and garnish with parsley. Serves 3 to 4.

SHRIMP CURRY

¾ c. flour
3½ T. curry powder
4 t. salt
½ t. ginger
2½ t. sugar
1 c. minced Bermuda onion
1 c. pared, diced apple
¾ c. butter
4 c. chicken broth
2 c. milk
3 T. butter
3 lbs. shrimp, shelled and deveined
1½ lbs. fresh mushroom caps, cleaned
¼ c. melted butter
2 T. lemon juice
2 c. cooked rice
  Minced parsley

Mix together the first 5 ingredients and set aside. Sauté onion and apple in ¾ cup butter until tender; blend in flour mixture. Slowly stir in broth and milk; simmer until thickened, stirring often. Remove from heat. Sauté shrimp in 3 tablespoons butter. Drain and add to curry sauce. Place mushroom caps in shallow pan and brush with melted butter; broil 3 minutes. Turn and brush with butter and broil another 3 minutes. Add to curry sauce with lemon juice. Can be refrigerated at this point. Before serving, reheat curry. Garnish with minced parsley. Serve over hot rice. Serves 8.

Pictured opposite:
Prawns in Envelopes

Shellfish

OYSTER SAUSAGES

½ lb. lean ground lamb
¼ lb. suet, finely chopped
1 c. coarsely chopped oysters with liquor
¼ c. light cream
¼ t. pepper
1 t. salt

Combine all ingredients, mixing well. Shape into rolls about the size of link sausages or make into small patties. Cover and fry over low heat in lightly greased skillet for 15 minutes. Remove cover, drain fat, and continue frying until brown. Serves 4.

MAINE CORN-OYSTER CASSEROLE

¼ lb. butter, melted
1 17-oz. can cream-style corn
1 17-oz. can whole kernel corn
1 c. milk
16 soda crackers, crushed
4 eggs, well beaten
1 12-oz. can cut-up oysters with liquor
Salt and pepper to taste

Mix all ingredients well and pour into a large deep casserole. Bake in a 350° oven until firm. Serves 4.

ESCALLOPED OYSTERS

½ c. stale bread crumbs
1 c. cracker crumbs
½ c. melted butter
1 pt. oysters
Salt and pepper to taste
4 T. bottled oyster sauce
2 T. milk

Mix bread and cracker crumbs; stir in butter. Line the bottom of a buttered baking dish with some of the buttered crumbs. Cover with half the oysters and sprinkle with salt and pepper. Combine sauce and milk; sprinkle half of liquid over oysters. Repeat with remaining oysters, liquid, and crumbs, ending with remaining bread crumbs. Bake in a 425° oven for 30 minutes. Serves 4.

OYSTER CHOP STEWY

5½ T. butter
1 c. thin onion wedges
1½ c. thin, diagonal celery slices
2 c. bean sprouts
1 c. teriyaki sauce
1 4-oz. can mushrooms, drained
1 pt. oysters and liquor
Dash of cayenne
Toast

Melt butter and sauté onions. Add celery, bean sprouts, and teriyaki sauce; simmer until celery is tender, stirring occasionally. Quickly sauté mushrooms in butter and add to vegetables; mix. Heat oysters in liquor; add to vegetables. Season with cayenne; serve hot with toast. Serves 6.

CHINESE OYSTER ROLL

15 oysters
  Hot water
 9 water chestnuts
 1 lb. ground pork
 4 fresh scallions, finely chopped
¼ c. finely chopped dry onion
½ t. salt
¼ t. monosodium glutamate
 2 eggs (1 egg well beaten)
  Cracker crumbs

Soak oysters overnight in hot water. Clean well; remove muscle; chop fine. Combine oysters, water chestnuts, pork, scallions, onions, salt, monosodium glutamate, and unbeaten egg. Mix thoroughly, and form into rolls ½-inch thick and 2-inches long. Dip in beaten egg, roll in cracker crumbs; fry in deep fat. Do not brown too quickly as pork must be well done; drain and serve hot. Serves 6 to 8.

BAKED OYSTERS DELUXE

12 oysters on the half shell
  Salt and pepper
 6 t. horseradish
¾ c. cracker crumbs
 1 T. melted butter

Season oysters with salt and pepper. Over each oyster, spread ½ teaspoon of horseradish. Mix cracker crumbs with butter and spread over oysters. Broil or bake in a 450° oven for 10 minutes or until browned. Serves 2.

OYSTERS CASINO

24 oysters on the half shell
  Lemon juice
1½ c. minced green pepper
  Bacon, chopped in 1-inch squares
  Salt and pepper

Over each oyster, sprinkle a few drops of lemon juice, 1 teaspoon green pepper, and a square of bacon. Sprinkle with pepper and salt. Bake in a 400° oven for 10 to 12 minutes or place under broiler for 5 minutes. Serves 4.

ABALONE HAWAIIAN STYLE

 4 dried mushrooms
  Water
 1 c. chicken broth
 1 1-lb. can abalone, cut in 1-inch pieces; reserve liquid
 1 c. green onions, cut in 1-inch slices
⅓ c. celery, diced
 6 water chestnuts, thinly sliced
1½ T. soy sauce
 1 T. white wine
 2 T. cornstarch

Cover mushrooms with water and soak for 2 hours. Drain and slice. Heat broth and abalone liquid; add vegetables and simmer 5 minutes. Add remaining ingredients and simmer until sauce is thick and clear. Serve with rice. Serves 4.

ABALONE WITH OYSTER SAUCE

 1 can abalone
  Blanched lettuce
  Blanched broccoli
 1 t. cornstarch
¼ c. juice from abalone
 2 T. salad oil
 1 T. cooking sherry
 2 T. chicken broth
 2 T. bottled oyster sauce
½ t. soy sauce
  Dash of sugar
 2 drops sesame oil

Slice the abalone into 1-inch pieces. Blanch lettuce by boiling for 1 minute and blanch broccoli by boiling 5 minutes. Mix together cornstarch and the juice from the abalone. Heat oil. Pour in sherry, broth, oyster sauce, soy sauce, and sugar. Boil for 5 minutes. Pour in cornstarch mixture, stirring until the juice thickens; add the sesame oil. Add abalone and boil an additional 30 seconds. Place abalone mixture on lettuce and broccoli. Serve immediately.

Note: Abalone will be tough if overcooked.

ESCARGOTS

24 escargot shells
⅓ lb. butter
1½ t. minced onion
1 t. minced garlic
½ T. parsley, chopped
   Salt and pepper
1 4½-oz. can snails
3 T. plum wine
   Fine cracker crumbs

Cream butter; add onion, garlic, parsley, salt and pepper; blend until smooth. Put a little in each shell, put a snail on top, and cover with remaining butter mixture. Arrange shells in baking dish; pour wine around shells; sprinkle cracker crumbs over. Bake in a 450° oven for 10 minutes. Serve immediately with clamp holders and snail forks. Serves 2 to 4.

SKEWERED SCALLOPS

1 lb. fresh scallops
4 T. prepared mustard
4 T. heavy cream
   Dry bread crumbs, finely crushed
   Cherry tomatoes
   Green pepper squares
   Salt, pepper, paprika
   Salad oil

Wash scallops in cold water and cut into ¾-inch pieces. Combine mustard and heavy cream; dip scallops in mustard mixture; then in bread crumbs, coating completely. Alternate scallops, tomatoes, and green peppers on skewers; sprinkle with salt, pepper, and paprika. Brush scallops and vegetables with salad oil. Grill over medium flame for 10 to 15 minutes until scallops are lightly browned. Serve with your favorite seafood sauce. Serves 4.

SCALLOPS WITH PEPPERS

2 T. salad oil
1 small onion, sliced into thin rounds
2 to 3 c. raw scallops, rinsed, drained and sliced into ¼-inch rounds
½ t. salt
¼ t. black pepper
3 green peppers, cut into 1-inch squares
1 T. sherry

Preheat wok on high for 30 seconds. Heat oil; add onion and stir-fry for 1 minute. Add scallops, toss to coat with oil, add salt and pepper; stir-fry 3 minutes; add green pepper and stir-fry 2 to 3 minutes; stir in sherry. Remove while peppers are still deep green. Serves 4 to 6.

CREAMED SCALLOPS

1 pt. scallops, fresh or canned
2 c. White Sauce (page 22)
   Rice
   Paprika

Make White Sauce. Wash and drain scallops; add to White Sauce and simmer 15 minutes in double boiler. Serve over steaming rice and sprinkle with paprika. Serves 2.

SAVORY SAUTÉED SCALLOPS

2 lbs. scallops, cut in squares
1 c. milk
½ c. flour
4½ T. vegetable oil
   Salt and pepper
   Juice of ½ lemon
6 t. butter
1 t. parsley
   Lemon wedges

Wash scallops, and dry. Dip in milk, then in flour. Heat oil until hot and sauté scallops, searing them quickly until brown. Remove to serving platter, season with salt and pepper and sprinkle lightly with lemon juice. Brown butter in pan; pour over scallops. Sprinkle with parsley and garnish with lemon wedges. Serves 4 to 6.

Pictured opposite:
Skewered Scallops

WHITE CLAM SAUCE SUPERB

2 T. olive oil or peanut oil
2 T. butter
1 small onion, minced
2 small cloves garlic, pressed
  Salt and pepper
¼ t. oregano
2 8-oz. cans minced clams, drain and
  reserve liquid
¾ lb. spaghetti, cooked
3 T. chopped parsley
  Parmesan cheese

Put oil, butter, onion, pressed garlic, salt
and pepper in pan. Sauté until golden brown.
Add oregano, drained clams and a little of
the clam juice. Cover and steam for 5 minutes on low heat. Pour over spaghetti,
sprinkle with chopped parsley and Parmesan
cheese. Serves 4.

EMMA'S CLAM FRITTERS

1½ c. sifted flour
2¼ t. baking powder
 ½ t. salt
 2 egg yolks
 ¾ c. milk
1½ T. salad oil
 1 egg white, beaten
 1 t. grated lemon rind
 2 3¾-oz. cans whole baby clams, drained
   Lemon wedges
   Tartar sauce

Sift flour with baking powder and salt. Beat
egg yolks, milk and oil until combined.
Gradually add flour mixture, beating until
smooth. Fold in egg white and lemon rind.
Dip clams in batter, coating evenly. Deep
fry a few at a time until browned; drain.
Serve hot with tartar sauce and lemon
wedges. Makes 24 fritters.

FISHERMAN'S SPAGHETTI

1 10-oz. can whole clams and liquid
1 8-oz. can minced clams and liquid
1 4½-oz. can shrimp and liquid
1 T. chopped onion
1 clove garlic, minced
½ c. white table wine
¼ lb. butter
3 dashes Tabasco
  Freshly ground pepper to taste
1 10½-oz. can cream sauce
1 lb. spaghetti, cooked
  Freshly grated Parmesan cheese
  Freshly chopped chives

In frying pan, sauté onion and garlic; do not
brown. Add wine and reduce heat to a
simmer. Add the seafood and butter; heat
until butter melts completely. Add Tabasco
sauce and freshly ground pepper. Add cream
sauce. Arrange spaghetti on a deep platter;
pour sauce over. Add a liberal amount of
grated Parmesan cheese. Sprinkle with
freshly chopped chives. Serves 4.

STEWED CLAMS

4 carrots, peeled and diced
1 c. peas, fresh or frozen
6 small new potatoes, peeled and diced
6 small white onions, peeled
4 stalks celery, sliced
1 8¾-oz. can cream-style corn
2 bay leaves
¼ t. basil
¼ t. rosemary
¼ t. thyme
1 10½-oz. can clam juice
4 8-oz. cans minced clams
1 c. butter
  Rounds of French bread, toasted

Combine all ingredients in a large pan or
Dutch oven, except clams, butter, and toast
rounds. Add enough water to barely cover
vegetables. Bring to a boil and simmer,
covered, until vegetables are tender. Add
clams and butter; heat to melt butter. Top
with toasted bread rounds. Serves 8 to 10.

Glossary

Drawn: Scaled and insides removed.

Dressed: Scaled and the head, tail and fins removed.

Fillets: The sides of small to medium fish cut lengthwise away from the backbone, usually boneless.

Steaks: Crosswise sections of large fish such as salmon. They are cut not less than 1 inch thick and contain a piece of backbone.

SHELLFISH:

Clams: Clams are sold by the dozen or quart. When purchased, the shells must be tightly closed. There are soft-shelled and hard-shelled clams. To help remove sand, place live clams in cold water to cover. Sprinkle oatmeal over the top, and let stand 2 to 3 hours before opening and cooking. Use a knife or steam to open.

Crab: Crab are sold by the dozen or pound. Soft-shelled crab are usually fried; hard-shelled ones are boiled, and the meat picked from them for use in various dishes.

Lobster: Live, plunge in boiling salted water. Boil 10 minutes, then simmer 25 minutes. Plunge in cold water and chill. Break off 2 large claws and 4 pairs of small ones. Separate tail and body joint. Cut a slit lengthwise through the center of the tail. Remove the black vein running down the back of tail meat. Remove stomach. The green portions are liver and roe; both are edible. Break open the claws and remove meat. If the lobster is frozen and to be broiled or baked, clean according to the above directions and cook according to recipe directions. You do not have to boil ahead of time.

Oysters: Oysters are sold by the dozen either in shells or shucked. Shells should be tightly closed when purchased. Shucked oysters should be plump, with no evidence of shrinkage. Examine oysters carefully and remove any pieces of shell that cling to them. Cook the oysters only long enough for the gills to curl.

Shrimp: Shrimp are bought by the pound with the heads removed. Raw shrimp are grayish-green in color and cooked shrimp are reddish. When purchased, shrimp should be firm-fleshed. The shell is parchment-like and easily removed. Shrimp is cooked in salted water. Bring water to a boil and cook 5 minutes. Cool, shell, and chill. With a sharp knife, remove the black vein down the back.

In these recipes saltwater fish can be substituted for one another, as can freshwater fish.

Fat fish have oil running through all the flesh. They are generally best for broiling, baking and planking.

Lean fish have drier flesh; they are best for boiling and steaming. When baked, add strips of bacon and when broiling, baste often with butter.

FRESHWATER FISH:		SALTWATER FISH:			
Carp	lean	Whitefish	fat	Pollock	lean
Catfish	lean	Yellow Perch	lean	Red Salmon	lean
Lake Trout	fat			Red Snapper	lean
Pike	lean	Cod	lean	Salmon	fat
Rainbow Trout	fat	Flounder or Sole	lean	Sea Bass	lean
Smelt	lean	Haddock	lean	Swordfish	lean
Sturgeon	fat	Halibut	lean	Tuna	fat
		Mullet	lean	Turbot	lean
				Whiting	lean

Index

Pictured opposite:
Stewed Clams, p. 60

Sauces

Beer Sauce, 22
Celery Sauce, 22
Chinese Barbecue Sauce for Fish, 21
Cucumber Sauce, 21
Dill Pickle Tartar Sauce, 21
Gala Seafood Cocktail Sauce, 22
Marinara Sauce for Fish, 22
Quick Hollandaise, 21
Seafood Cocktail Sauce, 21
Sour Cream-Dill Sauce, 22
Tasty Tartar Sauce, 21
White Sauce, 22
Yellow Sauce, 22

Shellfish

Abalone Hawaiian Style, 57
Abalone with Oyster Sauce, 57
Baked Oysters Deluxe, 57
Chinese Oyster Roll, 57
Creamed Scallops, 59
Emma's Clam Fritters, 60
Escalloped Oysters, 56
Escargots, 59
Fisherman's Spaghetti, 60
Maine Corn-Oyster Casserole, 56
Oyster Chop Stewy, 56
Oyster Sausages, 56
Oysters Casino, 57
Savory Sautéed Scallops, 59
Scallops with Peppers, 59
Skewered Scallops, 59
Stewed Clams, 60
White Clam Sauce Superb, 60

Soups

Chili of the Sea, 16
Codfish Chowder, 17
Crab Gumbo, 17
Elaine's Crab Soup, 16
Elegant Oyster Soup, 16
Fine Abalone Soup, 15
Haddock Soup, 17
Mock Bouillabaisse, 15
New England Clam Chowder, 16
Oyster Soup New Orleans, 17
Quick Clam Chowder, 17
Whaler's Tuna Chowder, 15

E F G H I J K L 1 2 3 4 5 6 7 8 9 0 1